FREE

Free Study Tips DVD

In addition to the tips and content in this guide, we have created a FREE DVD with helpful study tips to further assist your exam preparation. **This FREE Study Tips DVD provides you with top-notch tips to conquer your exam and reach your goals.**

Our simple request in exchange for the strategy-packed DVD is that you email us your feedback about our study guide. We would love to hear what you thought about the guide, and we welcome any and all feedback—positive, negative, or neutral. It is our #1 goal to provide you with top quality products and customer service.

To receive your **FREE Study Tips DVD**, email freedvd@apexprep.com. Please put "FREE DVD" in the subject line and put the following in the email:

a. The name of the study guide you purchased.

b. Your rating of the study guide on a scale of 1-5, with 5 being the highest score.

c. Any thoughts or feedback about your study guide.

d. Your first and last name and your mailing address, so we know where to send your free DVD!

Thank you!

ACCUPLACER Study Guide 2018 & 2019
ACCUPLACER 2018 & 2019 Prep & Practice Test Questions

APEX Test Prep College Placement Study Guide 2018-2019 Team

Table of Contents

Test Taking Strategies

1. Reading the Whole Question

A popular assumption in Western culture is the idea that we don't have enough time for anything. We speed while driving to work, we want to read an assignment for class as quickly as possible, or we want the line in the supermarket to dwindle faster. However, speeding through such events robs us from being able to thoroughly appreciate and understand what's happening around us. While taking a timed test, the feeling one might have while reading a question is to find the correct answer as quickly as possible. Although pace is important, don't let it deter you from reading the whole question. Test writers know how to subtly change a test question toward the end in various ways, such as adding a negative or changing focus. If the question has a passage, carefully read the whole passage as well before moving on to the questions. This will help you process the information in the passage rather than worrying about the questions you've just read and where to find them. A thorough understanding of the passage or question is an important way for test takers to be able to succeed on an exam.

2. Examining Every Answer Choice

Let's say we're at the market buying apples. The first apple we see on top of the heap may *look* like the best apple, but if we turn it over we can see bruising on the skin. We must examine several apples before deciding which apple is the best. Finding the correct answer choice is like finding the best apple. Some exams ask for the *best* answer choice, which means that there are several choices that could be correct, but one choice is always better than the rest. Although it's tempting to choose an answer that seems correct at first without reading the others, it's important to read each answer choice thoroughly before making a final decision on the answer. The aim of a test writer might be to get as close as possible to the correct answer, so watch out for subtle words that may indicate an answer is incorrect. Once the correct answer choice is selected, read the question again and the answer in response to make sure all your bases are covered.

3. Eliminating Wrong Answer Choices

Sometimes we become paralyzed when we are confronted with too many choices. Which frozen yogurt flavor is the tastiest? Which pair of shoes look the best with this outfit? What type of car will fill my needs as a consumer? If you are unsure of which answer would be the best to choose, it may help to use process of elimination. We use "filtering" all the time on sites such as eBay® or Craigslist® to eliminate the ads that are not right for us. We can do the same thing on an exam. Process of elimination is crossing out the answer choices we know for sure are wrong and leaving the ones that might be correct. It may help to cover up the incorrect answer choices with a piece of paper, although if the exam is computer-based, you may have to use your hand or mentally cross out the incorrect answer choices. Covering incorrect choices is a psychological act that alleviates stress due to the brain being exposed to a smaller amount of information. Choosing between two answer choices is much easier than choosing between four or five, and you have a better chance of selecting the correct answer if you have less to focus on.

4. Sticking to the World of the Question

When we are attempting to answer questions, our minds will often wander away from the question and what it is asking. We begin to see answer choices that are true in the real world instead of true in the world of the question. It may be helpful to think of each test question as its own little world. This world may be different from ours. This world may know as a truth that the chicken came before the egg or may assert that two plus two equals five. Remember that, no matter what hypothetical nonsense may be in the question, assume it to be true. If the question states that the chicken came before the egg, then choose your answer based on that truth. Sticking to the world of the question means placing all of our biases and assumptions aside and relying on the question to guide us to the correct answer. If we are simply looking for answers that are correct based on our own judgment, then we may choose incorrectly. Remember an answer that is true does not necessarily answer the question.

5. Key Words

If you come across a complex test question that you have to read over and over again, try pulling out some key words from the question in order to understand what exactly it is asking. Key words may be words that surround the question, such as *main idea, analogous, parallel, resembles, structured,* or *defines.* The question may be asking for the main idea, or it may be asking you to define something. Deconstructing the sentence may also be helpful in making the question simpler before trying to answer it. This means taking the sentence apart and obtaining meaning in pieces, or separating the question from the foundation of the question. For example, let's look at this question:

> Given the author's description of the content of paleontology in the first paragraph, which of the following is most parallel to what it taught?

The question asks which one of the answers most *parallels* the following information: The *description* of paleontology in the first paragraph. The first step would be to see *how* paleontology is described in the first paragraph. Then, we would find an answer choice that parallels that description. The question seems complex at first, but after we deconstruct it, the answer becomes much more attainable.

6. Subtle Negatives

Negative words in question stems will be words such as *not, but, neither,* or *except.* Test writers often use these words in order to trick unsuspecting test takers into selecting the wrong answer—or, at least, to test their reading comprehension of the question. Many exams will feature the negative words in all caps (*which of the following is NOT an example*), but some questions will add the negative word seamlessly into the sentence. The following is an example of a subtle negative used in a question stem:

> According to the passage, which of the following is *not* considered to be an example of paleontology?

If we rush through the exam, we might skip that tiny word, *not,* inside the question, and choose an answer that is opposite of the correct choice. Again, it's important to read the question fully, and double check for any words that may negate the statement in any way.

7. Spotting the Hedges

The word "hedging" refers to language that remains vague or avoids absolute terminology. Absolute terminology consists of words like *always, never, all, every, just, only, none,* and *must.* Hedging refers to words like *seem, tend, might, most, some, sometimes, perhaps, possibly, probability,* and *often.* In some cases, we want to choose answer choices that use hedging and avoid answer choices that use absolute terminology. Of course, this always depends on what subject you are being tested on. Humanities subjects like history and literature will contain hedging, because those subjects often do not have absolute answers. However, science and math may contain absolutes that are necessary for the question to be answered. It's important to pay attention to what subject you are on and adjust your response accordingly.

8. Restating to Understand

Every now and then we come across questions that we don't understand. The language may be too complex, or the question is structured in a way that is meant to confuse the test taker. When you come across a question like this, it may be worth your time to rewrite or restate the question in your own words in order to understand it better. For example, let's look at the following complicated question:

> Which of the following words, if substituted for the word *parochial* in the first paragraph, would LEAST change the meaning of the sentence?

Let's restate the question in order to understand it better. We know that they want the word *parochial* replaced. We also know that this new word would "least" or "not" change the meaning of the sentence. Now let's try the sentence again:

> Which word could we replace with *parochial,* and it would not change the meaning?

Restating it this way, we see that the question is asking for a synonym. Now, let's restate the question so we can answer it better:

> Which word is a synonym for the word *parochial*?

Before we even look at the answer choices, we have a simpler, restated version of a complicated question. Remember that, if you have paper, you can always rewrite the simpler version of the question so as not to forget it.

9. Guessing

When is it okay to guess on an exam? This question depends on the test format of the particular exam you're taking. On some tests, answer choices that are answered incorrectly are penalized. If you know that you are penalized for wrong answer choices, avoid guessing on the test question. If you can narrow the question down to fifty percent by process of elimination, then perhaps it may be worth it to guess between two answer choices. But if you are unsure of the correct answer choice among three or four answers, it may help to leave the question unanswered. Likewise, if the exam you are taking does *not* penalize for wrong answer choices, answer the questions first you know to be true, then go back through and mark an answer choice, even if you do not know the correct answer. This way, you will at least have a one in four chance of getting the answer correct. It may also be helpful to do some research on the exam you plan to take in order to understand how the questions are graded.

10. Avoiding Patterns

One popular myth in grade school relating to standardized testing is that test writers will often put multiple-choice answers in patterns. A runoff example of this kind of thinking is that the most common answer choice is "C," with "B" following close behind. Or, some will advocate certain made-up word patterns that simply do not exist. Test writers do not arrange their correct answer choices in any kind of pattern; their choices are randomized. There may even be times where the correct answer choice will be the same letter for two or three questions in a row, but we have no way of knowing when or if this might happen. Instead of trying to figure out what choice the test writer probably set as being correct, focus on what the *best answer choice* would be out of the answers you are presented with. Use the tips above, general knowledge, and reading comprehension skills in order to best answer the question, rather than looking for patterns that do not exist.

FREE DVD OFFER

Achieving a high score on your exam depends not only on understanding the content, but also on understanding how to apply your knowledge and your command of test taking strategies. **Because your success is our primary goal, we offer a FREE Study Tips DVD, which provides top-notch test taking strategies to help you optimize your testing experience.**

Our simple request in exchange for the strategy-packed DVD is that you email us your feedback about our study guide.

To receive your **FREE Study Tips DVD**, email freedvd@apexprep.com. Please put "FREE DVD" in the subject line and put the following in the email:

    a. The name of the study guide you purchased.

    b. Your rating of the study guide on a scale of 1-5, with 5 being the highest score.

    c. Any thoughts or feedback about your study guide.

    d. Your first and last name and your mailing address, so we know where to send your free DVD!

Introduction to the ACCUPLACER

Function of the Test

The ACCUPLACER is a computer assessment exam that tests reading, writing, and math skills for students hoping to enter secondary or postsecondary institutions. The exam has three integrated components built into it: placement assessments for the purpose of the test-taker finding a placement in an institution to align with course requirements, diagnostic assessments in the topics to see areas where they succeed or have knowledge gaps, and skill-building support in the topics used to improve skills in the topics and improve preparedness for college.

The exam tests preparedness for that specific institution in the three core subjects and is given by The College Board for the purposes of measuring where students are at academically in their studies. Schools that assess ACCUPLACER scores are community colleges, technical school, four-year universities, and high schools that use the scores for placement in their institutions. Over 2,000 institutions administer over 8.5 million exams each year to students.

Test Administration

The ACCUPLACER is typically given by appointment through the college or institution's advising and counseling office, though they offer testing alternatives if you live far away from a school or university. Those who do poorly on the exam have the option to retest seven days after the first exam is complete, although they may not exceed five retests in a year's time. Disability accommodations will be handled by the institution's testing center.

Test Format

The test will be given at a local college campus or school, so each testing environment for the ACCUPLACER will be different. Bring a photo ID and any other materials suggested by your institution. If the school you want to attend is located in a different area, your school should have remote options available to you.

The testing format is multiple-choice with no time limit. Keep in mind that with the computer-based assessment, each test question you answer correctly will make the next question more difficult, and each question you answer incorrectly will make the next question easier. With that said, do not rush through this exam, but give each question your undivided attention. The following bullet points show each section of the test and the types of questions in each. Each section has at least 12 questions but no more than 40.

- Arithmetic section: Operations with whole numbers and fractions, operations with decimals and percents, and applications and problem solving.

- College-Level Math section: Algebra operations, solutions of equations and inequalities, coordinate geometry, applications and other algebra topics, and functions and trigonometry

- Elementary Algebra section: Operations with integers and rational numbers; operations with algebraic expressions; solution of equations, inequalities, and word problems

- Reading Comprehension section: Understanding what's been read, making inferences, identifying main ideas, and distinguishing between direct statements or supporting ideas

- Sentence Skills section: Sentence structure, logic of a sentence, relationships between sentences

- Writeplacer section: Measures ability to write effectively, specifically looking at focus, organization, development and support, sentence structure, and mechanical conventions

Scoring

As soon as you are finished with the ACCUPLACER exam, the score reporting is instantly reported back to you. The ACCUPLACER Math and English sections are graded on scales that range from 20 to 120 points. The Writeplacer is scored between 0 and 8 points. The scores are used by college counselors to place you in the appropriate college courses, or by the admissions office for admission purposes. Score results are available to you for four years.

Arithmetic

Operations with Whole Numbers and Fractions

Addition, Subtraction, Multiplication, and Division

The four basic operations include addition, subtraction, multiplication, and division. The result of addition is a sum, the result of subtraction is a difference, the result of multiplication is a product, and the result of division is a quotient. Each type of operation can be used when working with rational numbers; however, the basic operations need to be understood first while using simpler numbers before working with fractions and decimals.

Performing these operations should first be learned using whole numbers. Addition needs to be done column by column. To add two whole numbers, add the ones column first, then the tens columns, then the hundreds, etc. If the sum of any column is greater than 9, a one must be carried over to the next column. For example, the following is the result of 482+924:

$$\begin{array}{r} 1 \\ 482 \\ +924 \\ \hline 1406 \end{array}$$

Notice that the sum of the tens column was 10, so a one was carried over to the hundreds column. Subtraction is also performed column by column. Subtraction is performed in the ones column first, then the tens, etc. If the number on top is smaller than the number below, a one must be borrowed from the column to the left. For example, the following is the result of 5,424 − 756:

$$\begin{array}{r} 4\ 13\ 11\ 14 \\ \cancel{5}\ \cancel{4}\ \cancel{2}\ \cancel{4} \\ -\ 7\ \ 5\ \ 6 \\ \hline 4\ \ 6\ \ 6\ \ 8 \end{array}$$

Notice that a one is borrowed from the tens, hundreds, and thousands place. After subtraction, the answer can be checked through addition. A check of this problem would be to show that 756+4,668 = 5,424.

Multiplication of two whole numbers is performed by writing one on top of the other. The number on top is known as the *multiplicand,* and the number below is the *multiplier.* Perform the multiplication by multiplying the multiplicand by each digit of the multiplier. Make sure to place the ones value of each result under the multiplying digit in the multiplier. Each value to the right is then a 0. The product is found by adding each product. For example, the following is the process of multiplying 46 times 37 where 46 is the multiplicand and 37 is the multiplier:

Finally, division can be performed using long division. When dividing a number by another number, the first number is known as the *dividend*, and the second is the *divisor*. For example, with $a \div b = c$, a is the dividend, b is the divisor, and c is the quotient. For long division, place the dividend within the division symbol and the divisor on the outside. For example, with $8,764 \div 4$, refer to the first problem in the diagram below. First, there are two 4's in the first digit, 8. This number 2 gets written above the 8. Then, multiply 4 times 2 to get 8, and that product goes below the 8. Subtract to get 8, and then carry down the 7. Continue the same steps. $7 \div 4 = 1$ R3, so 1 is written above the 7. Multiply 4 times 1 to get 4 and write it below the 7. Subtract to get 3 and carry the 6 down next to the 3. The resulting steps give a 9 and a 1. The final subtraction results in a 0, which means that 8,764 is divisible by 4. There are no remaining numbers.

The second example shows that $4,536 \div 216 = 21$. The steps are a little different because 216 cannot be contained in 4 or 5, so the first step is placing a 2 above the 3 because there are two 216's in 453. Finally, the third example shows that $546 \div 31 = 17$ R19. The 19 is a remainder. Notice that the final subtraction does not result in a 0, which means that 546 is not divisible by 31. The remainder can also be written as a fraction over the divisor to say that $546 \div 31 = 17\frac{19}{31}$.

```
    2 1 9 1            2 1            1 7  r  1 9
  4 | 8 7 6 4      216 | 4 5 3 6    31 | 5 4 6
    8                   4 3 2            3 1
    0 7                 2 1 6            2 3 6
    4                   2 1 6            2 1 7
    3 6                     0             1 9
    3 6
    0 4
      4
      0
```

If a division problem relates to a real-world application, and a remainder does exist, it can have meaning. For example, consider the third example, $546 \div 31 = 17$ R19. Let's say that we had $546 to spend on calculators that cost $31 each, and we wanted to know how many we could buy. The division problem would answer this question. The result states that 17 calculators could be purchased, with $19 left over. Notice that the remainder will never be greater than or equal to the divisor.

Once the operations are understood with whole numbers, they can be used with integers. There are many rules surrounding operations with negative numbers. First, consider addition with integers. The sum of two numbers can first be shown using a number line. For example, to add $-5 + (-6)$, plot the point -5 on the number line. Then, because a negative number is being added, move 6 units to the left. This process results in landing on -11 on the number line, which is the sum of -5 and -6. If adding a positive number, move to the right. Visualizing this process using a number line is useful for understanding; however, it is not efficient. A quicker process is to learn the rules. When adding two numbers with the same sign, add the absolute values of both numbers, and use the common sign of both numbers as the sign of the sum. For example, to add $-5 + (-6)$, add their absolute values $5 + 6 = 11$. Then, introduce a negative number because both addends are negative. The result is -11. To add two integers with unlike signs, subtract the lesser absolute value from the greater absolute value, and apply the sign of the number with the greater absolute value to the result. For example, the sum $-7 + 4$ can be computed by finding the difference $7 - 4 = 3$ and then applying a negative because the value with the larger absolute value is negative. The result is -3. Similarly, the sum $-4 + 7$ can be found by computing the same difference but leaving it as a positive result because the addend with the larger absolute value is positive. Also, recall that any number plus 0 equals that number. This is known as the *Addition Property of 0*.

Subtracting two integers can be computed by changing to addition to avoid confusion. The rule is to add the first number to the opposite of the second number. The opposite of a number is the number on the other side of 0 on the number line, which is the same number of units away from 0. For example, -2 and 2 are opposites. Consider $4 - 8$. Change this to adding the opposite as follows: $4 + (-8)$. Then, follow the rules of addition of integers to obtain -4. Secondly, consider $-8 - (-2)$. Change this problem to adding the opposite as $-8 + 2$, which equals -6. Notice that subtracting a negative number is really adding a positive number.

Multiplication and division of integers are actually less confusing than addition and subtraction because the rules are simpler to understand. If two factors in a multiplication problem have the same sign, the result is positive. If one factor is positive and one factor is negative, the result, known as the *product*, is negative. For example, $(-9)(-3) = 27$ and $9(-3) = -27$. Also, a number times 0 always results in 0. If a problem consists of more than a single multiplication, the result is negative if it contains an odd number of negative factors, and the result is positive if it contains an even number of negative factors. For example, $(-1)(-1)(-1)(-1) = 1$ and $(-1)(-1)(-1)(-1)(-1) = -1$. A similar theory applies within division. First, consider some vocabulary. When dividing 14 by 2, it can be written in the following ways: $14 \div 2 = 7$ or $\frac{14}{2} = 7$. 14 is the *dividend*, 2 is the *divisor*, and 7 is the *quotient*. If two numbers in a division problem have the same sign, the quotient is positive. If two numbers in a division problem have different signs, the quotient is negative. For example, $14 \div (-2) = -7$, and $-14 \div (-2) = 7$. To check division, multiply the quotient times the divisor to obtain the dividend. Also, remember that 0 divided by any number is equal to 0. However, any number divided by 0 is undefined. It just does not make sense to divide a number by 0 parts.

If more than one operation is to be completed in a problem, follow the Order of Operations. The mnemonic device, PEMDAS, for the order of operations states the order in which addition, subtraction, multiplication, and division needs to be done. It also includes when to evaluate operations within grouping symbols and when to incorporate exponents. PEMDAS, which some remember by thinking "please excuse my dear Aunt Sally," refers to parentheses, exponents, multiplication, division, addition, and subtraction. First, within an expression, complete any operation that is within parentheses, or any other grouping symbol like brackets, braces, or absolute value symbols. Note that this does not refer to the case when parentheses are used to represent multiplication like (2)(5). An operation is not within parentheses like it is in (2 × 5). Then, any exponents must be computed. Next, multiplication and division are performed from left to right. Finally, addition and subtraction are performed from left to right. The following is an example in which the operations within the parentheses need to be performed first, so the order of operations must be applied to the exponent, subtraction, addition, and multiplication within the grouping symbol:

$$9 - 3(3^2 - 3 + 4 \cdot 3)$$

$$9 - 3(3^2 - 3 + 4 \cdot 3) \quad \text{Work within the parentheses first}$$

$$= 9 - 3(9 - 3 + 12)$$

$$= 9 - 3(18)$$

$$= 9 - 54$$

$$= -45$$

Interpreting Remainders in Division Problems

Understanding remainders begins with understanding the division problem. The problem 24 ÷ 7 can be read as "twenty-four divided by seven." The problem is asking how many groups of 7 will fit into 24. Counting by seven, the multiples are 7, 14, 21, 28. Twenty-one, which is three groups of 7, is the closest to 24. The difference between 21 and 24 is 3, which is called the remainder. This is a remainder because it is the number that is left out after the three groups of seven are taken from 24. The answer to this division problem can be written as 3 with a remainder 3, or $3\frac{3}{7}$. The fraction $\frac{3}{7}$ can be used because it shows the part of the whole left when the division is complete. Another division problem may have the following numbers: 36 ÷ 5. This problem is asking how many groups of 5 will fit evenly into 36. When counting by multiples of 5, the following list is generated: 5, 10, 15, 20, 25, 30, 35, 40. As seen in the list, there are six groups of five that make 35. To get to the total of 36, there needs to be one additional number. The answer to the division problem would be 36 ÷ 5 = 6R1, or $6\frac{1}{5}$. The fractional part represents the number that cannot make up a whole group of five.

Recognizing Equivalent Fractions and Mixed Numbers

Within the number system, different forms of numbers can be used. It is important to be able to recognize each type, as well as work with, and convert between, the given forms. The *real number system* comprises natural numbers, whole numbers, integers, rational numbers, and irrational numbers. Natural numbers, whole numbers, integers, and irrational numbers typically are not represented as fractions, decimals, or percentages. Rational numbers, however, can be represented as any of these three forms. A *rational number* is a number that can be written in the form $\frac{a}{b}$, where a and b are integers, and b is not equal to zero. In other words, rational numbers can be written in a fraction form. The value a is the *numerator*, and b is the *denominator*. If the numerator is equal to zero, the entire fraction is equal to zero. Non-negative fractions can be less than 1, equal to 1, or greater than 1. Fractions are less than 1 if the numerator is smaller (less than) than the denominator. For example, $\frac{3}{4}$ is less than 1. A fraction is equal to 1 if the numerator is equal to the denominator. For instance, $\frac{4}{4}$ is equal to 1. Finally, a fraction is greater than 1 if the numerator is greater than the denominator: the fraction $\frac{11}{4}$ is greater than 1. When the numerator is greater than the denominator, the fraction is called an *improper fraction*. An improper fraction can be converted to a *mixed number*, a combination of both a whole number and a fraction. To convert an improper fraction to a mixed number, divide the numerator by the denominator. Write down the whole number portion, and then write any remainder over the original denominator. For example, $\frac{11}{4}$ is equivalent to $2\frac{3}{4}$. Conversely, a mixed number can be converted to an improper fraction by multiplying the denominator times the whole number and adding that result to the numerator.

Estimating

Sometimes it is helpful to find an estimated answer to a problem rather than working out an exact answer. An estimation might be much quicker to find, and given the scenario, an estimation might be all that is required. For example, if Aria goes grocery shopping and has only a $100 bill to cover all of her purchases, it might be appropriate for her to estimate the total of the items she is purchasing to tell if she has enough money to cover them. Also, an estimation can help determine if an answer makes sense. For instance, if an answer in the 100s is expected, but the result is a fraction less than 1, something is probably wrong in the calculation.

The first type of estimation involves rounding. *Rounding* consists of expressing a number in terms of the nearest decimal place like the tenth, hundredth, or thousandth place, or in terms of the nearest whole number unit like tens, hundreds, or thousands place. When rounding to a specific place value, look at the digit to the right of the place. If it is 5 or higher, round the number to its left up to the next value, and if it is 4 or lower, keep that number at the same value. For instance, 1,654.2674 rounded to the nearest thousand is 2,000, and the same number rounded to the nearest thousandth is 1,654.267. Rounding can be used in the scenario when grocery totals need to be estimated. Items can be rounded to the nearest dollar. For example, a can of corn that costs $0.79 can be rounded to $1.00, and then all other items can be rounded in a similar manner and added together. When working with larger numbers, it might make more sense to round to higher place values. For example, when estimating the total value of a dealership's car inventory, it would make sense to round the car values to the nearest thousands place. The price of a car that is on sale for $15,654 can be estimated at $16,000. All other cars on the lot could be rounded in the same manner, and then their sum can be found. Depending on the situation, it might make sense to calculate an over-estimate. For example, to make sure Aria has enough money at the grocery store, rounding up every time for each item would ensure that she will have enough money when it comes time to pay. A $.40 item rounded up to $1.00 would ensure that there is a dollar to cover that item. Traditional rounding rules would round $0.40 to $0, which does not make sense in this particular real-world setting. Aria might not have a dollar available at checkout to pay for that item if she uses traditional rounding. It is up to the customer to decide the best approach when estimating.

Estimating is also very helpful when working with measurements. Bryan is updating his kitchen and wants to retile the floor. Again, an over-measurement might be useful. Also, rounding to nearest half-unit might be helpful. For instance, one side of the kitchen might have an exact measurement of 14.32 feet, and the most useful measurement needed to buy tile could be estimating this quantity to be 14.5 feet. If the kitchen was rectangular and the other side measured 10.9 feet, Bryan might round the other side to 11 feet. Therefore, Bryan would find the total tile necessary according to the following area calculation: $14.5 \times 11 = 159.5$ square feet. To make sure he purchases enough tile, Bryan would probably want to purchase at least 160 square feet of tile. This is a scenario in which an estimation might be more useful than an exact calculation. Having more tile than necessary is better than having an exact amount, in case any tiles are broken or otherwise unusable.

Finally, estimation is helpful when exact answers are necessary. Consider a situation in which Sabina has many operations to perform on numbers with decimals, and she is allowed a calculator to find the result. Even though an exact result can be obtained with a calculator, there is always a possibility that Sabina could make an error while inputting the data. For example, she could miss a decimal place, or misuse a parenthesis, causing a problem with the actual order of operations. In this case, a quick estimation at the beginning would be helpful to make sure the final answer is given with the correct number of units. Sabina has to find the exact total of 10 cars listed for sale at the dealership. Each price has two decimal places included to account for both dollars and cents. If one car is listed at $21, 234.43 but Sabina incorrectly inputs into the calculator the price of $2,123.443, this error would throw off the final sum by almost $20,000. A quick estimation at the beginning, by rounding each price to the nearest thousands place and finding the sum of the prices, would give Sabina an amount to compare the exact amount to. This comparison would let Sabina see if an error was made in her exact calculation.

Operations with Decimals and Percents

Addition, Subtraction, Multiplication, and Division with Decimals

Operations can be performed on rational numbers in decimal form. Recall that to write a fraction as an equivalent decimal expression, divide the numerator by the denominator. For example, $\frac{1}{8} = 1 \div 8 = 0.125$. With the case of decimals, it is important to keep track of place value. To add decimals, make sure the decimal places are in alignment so that the numbers are lined up with their decimal points and add vertically. If the numbers do not line up because there are extra or missing place values in one of the numbers, then zeros may be used as placeholders. For example, $0.123 + 0.23$ becomes:

$$0.123$$
$$\underline{0.230}$$
$$0.353$$

Subtraction is done the same way. Multiplication and division are more complicated. To multiply two decimals, place one on top of the other as in a regular multiplication process and do not worry about lining up the decimal points. Then, multiply as with whole numbers, ignoring the decimals. Finally, in the solution, insert the decimal point as many places to the left as there are total decimal values in the original problem. Here is an example of a decimal multiplication:

$$
\begin{array}{rl}
0.52 & \textit{2 decimal places} \\
\times \quad 0.2 & \textit{1 decimal place} \\
\hline
0.104 & \textit{3 decimal places}
\end{array}
$$

The answer to 67 times 4 is 268, and because there are three decimal values in the problem, the decimal point is positioned three units to the left in the answer.

The decimal point plays an integral role throughout the whole problem when dividing with decimals. First, set up the problem in a long division format. If the divisor is not an integer, the decimal must be moved to the right as many units as needed to make it an integer. The decimal in the dividend must be moved to the right the same number of places to maintain equality. Then, division is completed normally. Here is an example of long division with decimals:

**Long division
with decimals**

Because the decimal point is moved two units to the right in the divisor of 0.06 to turn it into the integer 6, it is also moved two units to the right in the dividend of 12.72 to make it 1,272. The result is 212, and remember that a division problem can always be checked by multiplying the answer times the divisor to see if the result is equal to the dividend.

Sometimes it is helpful to round answers that are in decimal form. First, find the place to which the rounding needs to be done. Then, look at the digit to the right of it. If that digit is 4 or less, the number in the place value to its left stays the same, and everything to its right becomes a 0. This process is known as *rounding down*. If that digit is 5 or higher, round up by increasing the place value to its left by 1, and every number to its right becomes a 0. If those 0's are in decimals, they can be dropped. For example, 0.145 rounded to the nearest hundredth place would be rounded up to 0.15, and 0.145 rounded to the nearest tenth place would be rounded down to 0.1.

Percent Problems

Percentages are defined to be parts per one hundred. To convert a decimal to a percentage, move the decimal point two units to the right and place the percent sign after the number. Percentages appear in many scenarios in the real world. It is important to make sure the statement containing the percentage is translated to a correct mathematical expression. Be aware that it is extremely common to make a mistake when working with percentages within word problems.

An example of a word problem containing a percentage is the following: 35% of people speed when driving to work. In a group of 5,600 commuters, how many would be expected to speed on the way to their place of employment? The answer to this problem is found by finding 35% of 5,600. First, change the percentage to the decimal 0.35. Then compute the product: $0.35 \times 5,600 = 1,960$. Therefore, it would be expected that 1,960 of those commuters would speed on their way to work based on the data given. In this situation, the word "of" signals to use multiplication to find the answer. Another way percentages are used is in the following problem: Teachers work 8 months out of the year. What percent of the year do they work? To answer this problem, find what percent of 12 the number 8 is, because there are 12 months in a year. Therefore, divide 8 by 12, and convert that number to a percentage: $\frac{8}{12} = \frac{2}{3} = 0.66\overline{6}$. The percentage rounded to the nearest tenth place tells us that teachers work 66.7% of the year. Percentages also appear in real-world application problems involving finding missing quantities like in the following question: 60% of what number is 75? To find the missing quantity, an equation can be used. Let x be equal to the missing quantity. Therefore, $0.60x = 75$. Divide each side by 0.60 to obtain 125. Therefore, 60% of 125 is equal to 75.

Sales tax is an important application relating to percentages because tax rates are usually given as percentages. For example, a city might have an 8% sales tax rate. Therefore, when an item is purchased with that tax rate, the real cost to the customer is 1.08 times the price in the store. For example, a $25 pair of jeans costs the customer $25 \times 1.08 = $27. Sales tax rates can also be determined if they are unknown when an item is purchased. If a customer visits a store and purchases an item for $21.44, but the price in the store was $19, they can find the tax rate by first subtracting $21.44 − $19 to obtain $2.44, the sales tax amount. The sales tax is a percentage of the in-store price. Therefore, the tax rate is $\frac{2.44}{19} = 0.128$, which has been rounded to the nearest thousandths place. In this scenario, the actual sales tax rate given as a percentage is 12.8%.

Recognition of Decimals

A *decimal* is a number that uses a decimal point and numbers to the right of the decimal point representing the part of the number that is less than 1. For example, 3.5 is a decimal and is equivalent to the fraction $\frac{7}{2}$ or mixed number $3\frac{1}{2}$. The decimal is found by dividing 2 into 7. Other examples of fractions are $\frac{2}{7}, \frac{-3}{14}$, and $\frac{14}{27}$.

Fractions can be converted to decimals. With a calculator, a fraction is converted to a decimal by dividing the numerator by the denominator. For example, $\frac{2}{5} = 2 \div 5 = 0.4$. Sometimes, rounding might be necessary. Consider $\frac{2}{7} = 2 \div 7 = 0.28571429$. This decimal could be rounded for ease of use, and if it needed to be rounded to the nearest thousandth, the result would be 0.286. If a calculator is not available, a fraction can be converted to a decimal manually. First, find a number that, when multiplied by the denominator, has a value equal to 10, 100, 1,000, etc. Then, multiply both the numerator and denominator times that number. The decimal form of the fraction is equal to the new numerator with a decimal point placed as many place values to the left as there are zeros in the denominator. For example, to convert $\frac{3}{5}$ to a decimal, multiply both the numerator and denominator times 2, which results in $\frac{6}{10}$. The decimal is equal to 0.6 because there is one zero in the denominator, and so the decimal place in the numerator is moved one unit to the left. In the case where rounding would be necessary while working without a calculator, an approximation must be found. A number close to 10, 100, 1,000, etc. can be used. For example, to convert $\frac{1}{3}$ to a decimal, the numerator and denominator can be multiplied by 33 to turn the denominator into approximately 100, which makes for an easier conversion to the equivalent decimal. This process results in $\frac{33}{99}$ and an approximate decimal of 0.33. Once in decimal form, the number can be converted to a percentage. Multiply the decimal by 100 and then place a percent sign after the number. For example, .614 is equal to 61.4%. In other words, move the decimal place two units to the right and add the percentage symbol.

Fraction and Percent Equivalencies

Fractions appear in everyday situations, and in many scenarios, they appear in the real-world as ratios and in proportions. A *ratio* is formed when two different quantities are compared. For example, in a group of 50 people, if there are 33 females and 17 males, the ratio of females to males is 33 to 17. This expression can be written in the fraction form, $\frac{33}{17}$, or by using the ratio symbol, 33:17. The order of the number matters when forming ratios. In the same setting, the ratio of males to females is 17 to 33, which is equivalent to $\frac{17}{33}$ or 17:33. A *proportion* is an equation involving two ratios. The equation $\frac{a}{b} = \frac{c}{d}$, or $a{:}b = c{:}d$ is a proportion, for real numbers a, b, c, and d. Usually, in one ratio, one of the quantities is unknown, and cross-multiplication is used to solve for the unknown. Consider $\frac{1}{4} = \frac{x}{5}$. To solve for x, cross-multiply to obtain $5 = 4x$. Divide each side by 4 to obtain the solution $x = \frac{5}{4}$. It is also true that percentages are ratios in which the second term is 100. For example, 65% is 65:100 or $\frac{65}{100}$. Therefore, when working with percentages, one is also working with ratios.

Applications and Problem Solving

Rate, Percent, and Measurement Problems

Real-world problems frequently involve proportions. For example, consider the following problem: If 2 out of 50 pizzas are usually delivered late from a local Italian restaurant, how many would be late out of 235 orders? The following proportion would be solved with x as the unknown quantity of late pizzas: $\frac{2}{50} = \frac{x}{235}$. Cross multiplying results in $470 = 50x$. Divide both sides by 50 to obtain $x = \frac{470}{50}$, which in lowest terms is equal to $\frac{47}{5}$. In decimal form, this improper fraction is equal to 9.4. Because it does not make sense to answer this question with decimals (portions of pizzas do not get delivered) the answer must be rounded. Traditional rounding rules would say that 9 pizzas would be expected to be delivered late. However, to be safe, rounding up to 10 pizzas out of 235 would probably make more sense.

Recall that a ratio is the comparison of two different quantities. Comparing 2 apples to 3 oranges results in the ratio 2:3, which can be expressed as the fraction $\frac{2}{3}$. Note that order is important when discussing ratios. The number mentioned first is the numerator, and the number mentioned second is the denominator. The ratio 2:3 does not mean the same quantity as the ratio 3:2. Also, it is important to make sure that when discussing ratios that have units attached to them, the two quantities use the same units. For example, to think of 8 feet to 4 yards, it would make sense to convert 4 yards to feet by multiplying by 3. Therefore, the ratio would be 8 feet to 12 feet, which can be expressed as the fraction $\frac{8}{12}$. Also, note that it is proper to refer to ratios in lowest terms. Therefore, the ratio of 8 feet to 4 yards is equivalent to the fraction $\frac{2}{3}$. Many real-world problems involve ratios. Often, problems with ratios involve proportions, as when two ratios are set equal to find the missing amount. However, some problems involve deciphering single ratios. For example, consider an amusement park that sold 345 tickets last Saturday. If 145 tickets were sold to adults and the rest of the tickets were sold to children, what would the ratio of the number of adult tickets to children's tickets be? A common mistake would be to say the ratio is 145:345. However, 345 is the total number of tickets sold. There were 345 − 145 = 200 tickets sold to children. The correct ratio of adult to children's tickets is 145:200. As a fraction, this expression is written as $\frac{145}{200}$, which can be reduced to $\frac{29}{40}$.

While a ratio compares two measurements using the same units, rates compare two measurements with different units. Examples of rates would be $200 of work for 8 hours, or 500 miles per 20 gallons. Because the units are different, it is important to always include the units when discussing rates. Rates can be easily seen because if they are expressed in words, the two quantities are usually split up using one of the following words: *for, per, on, from, in*. Just as with ratios, it is important to write rates in lowest terms. A common rate that can be found in many real-life situations is cost per unit. This quantity describes how much one item or one unit costs. This rate allows the best buy to be determined, given a couple of different sizes of an item with different costs. For example, if 2 quarts of soup were sold for $3.50 and 3 quarts were sold for $4.60, to determine the best buy, the cost per quart should be found. $\frac{\$3.50}{2} = \$1.75$ per quart, and $\frac{\$4.60}{3} = \$1.53$ per quart. Therefore, the better deal would be the 3-quart option.

Rate of change problems involve calculating a quantity per some unit of measurement. Usually the unit of measurement is time. For example, meters per second is a common rate of change. To calculate this measurement, find the amount traveled in meters and divide by total time traveled. The calculation is an average of the speed over the entire time interval. Another common rate of change used in the real world is miles per hour. Consider the following problem that involves calculating an average rate of change in temperature. Last Saturday, the temperature at 1:00 a.m. was 34 degrees Fahrenheit, and at noon, the temperature had increased to 75 degrees Fahrenheit. What was the average rate of change over that time interval? The average rate of change is calculated by finding the change in temperature and dividing by the total hours elapsed. Therefore, the rate of change was equal to $\frac{75-34}{12-1} = \frac{41}{11}$ degrees per hour. This quantity rounded to two decimal places is equal to 3.72 degrees per hour.

A common rate of change that appears in algebra is the slope calculation. Given a linear equation in one variable, $y = mx + b$, the slope, m, is equal to $\frac{rise}{run}$ or $\frac{change\ in\ y}{change\ in\ x}$. In other words, slope is equivalent to the ratio of the vertical and horizontal changes between any two points on a line. The vertical change is known as the *rise*, and the horizontal change is known as the *run*. Given any two points on a line (x_1, y_1) and (x_2, y_2), slope can be calculated with the formula $m = \frac{y_2-y_1}{x_2-x_1} = \frac{\Delta y}{\Delta x}$. Common real-world applications of slope include determining how steep a staircase should be, calculating how steep a road is, and determining how to build a wheelchair ramp.

Many times, problems involving rates and ratios involve proportions. A proportion states that two ratios (or rates) are equal. The property of cross products can be used to determine if a proportion is true, meaning both ratios are equivalent. If $\frac{a}{b} = \frac{c}{d}$, then to clear the fractions, multiply both sides times the least common denominator, bd. This results in $ac = cd$, which is equal to the result of multiplying along both diagonals. For example, $\frac{4}{40} = \frac{1}{10}$ grants the cross product $4 \times 10 = 40 \times 1$. $40 = 40$ shows that this proportion is true. Cross products are used when proportions are involved in real-world problems. Consider the following: If 3 pounds of fertilizer will cover 75 square feet of grass, how many pounds are needed for 375 square feet? To solve this problem, a proportion can be set up using two ratios. Let x equal the unknown quantity, pounds needed for 375 feet. Then, the equation found by setting the two given ratios equal to one another is $\frac{3}{75} = \frac{x}{375}$. Cross multiplication gives $3 \times 375 = 75x$. Therefore, $1,125 = 75x$. Divide both sides by 75 to get $x = 15$. Therefore, 15 gallons of fertilizer is needed to cover 75 square feet of grass.

Measuring and Comparing Lengths of Objects Using Standard Tools
Lengths of objects can be measured using tools such as rulers, yard sticks, meter sticks, and tape measures. Typically, a ruler measures 12 inches, or one foot. For this reason, a ruler is normally used to measure lengths smaller than or just slightly more than 12 inches. Rulers may represent centimeters instead of inches. Some rulers have inches on one side and centimeters on the other. Be sure to recognize what units you are measuring in. The standard ruler measurements are divided into units of 1 inch and

normally broken down to $\frac{1}{2}, \frac{1}{4}, \frac{1}{8}$, and even $\frac{1}{16}$ of an inch for more precise measurements. If measuring in centimeters, the centimeter is likely divided into tenths. To measure the size of a picture, for purposes of buying a frame, a ruler is helpful. If the picture is very large, a yardstick, which measures 3 feet and normally is divided into feet and inches, might be useful. Using metric units, the meter stick measures 1 meter and is divided into 100 centimeters. To measure the size of a window in a home, either a yardstick or meter stick would work. To measure the size of a room, though, a tape measure would be the easiest tool to use. Tape measures can measure up to 10 feet, 25 feet, or more.

Converting Within and Between Standard and Metric Systems

When working with dimensions, sometimes the given units don't match the formula, and conversions must be made. The metric system has base units of meter for length, kilogram for mass, and liter for liquid volume. This system expands to three places above the base unit and three places below. These places correspond with prefixes with a base of 10.

The following table shows the conversions:

kilo-	hecto-	deka-	base	deci-	centi-	milli-
1,000 times the base	100 times the base	10 times the base		1/10 times the base	1/100 times the base	1/1000 times the base

To convert between units within the metric system, values with a base ten can be multiplied. The decimal can also be moved in the direction of the new unit by the same number of zeros on the number. For example, 3 meters is equivalent to .003 kilometers. The decimal moved three places (the same number of zeros for kilo-) to the left (the same direction from base to kilo-). Three meters is also equivalent to 3,000 millimeters. The decimal is moved three places to the right because the prefix milli- is three places to the right of the base unit.

The English Standard system used in the United States has a base unit of foot for length, pound for weight, and gallon for liquid volume. These conversions aren't as easy as the metric system because they aren't a base ten model. The following table shows the conversions within this system.

Length

1 foot (ft) = 12 inches (in)
1 yard (yd) = 3 feet
1 mile (mi) = 5280 feet
1 mile = 1760 yards

Weight

1 pound (lb) = 16 ounces (oz)
1 ton = 2000 pounds

Capacity

1 tablespoon (tbsp) = 3 teaspoons (tsp)
1 cup (c) = 16 tablespoons
1 cup = 8 fluid ounces (oz)
1 pint (pt) = 2 cups
1 quart (qt) = 2 pints
1 gallon (gal) = 4 quarts

When converting within the English Standard system, most calculations include a conversion to the base unit and then another to the desired unit. For example, take the following problem: 3 *quarts* = ___ *cups*. There is no straight conversion from quarts to cups, so the first conversion is from quarts to pints. There are 2 pints in 1 quart, so there are 6 pints in 3 quarts. This conversion can be solved as a proportion: $\frac{3\ qt}{x} = \frac{1\ qt}{2\ pints}$. It can also be observed as a ratio 2:1, expanded to 6:3. Then the 6 pints must be converted to cups. The ratio of pints to cups is 1:2, so the expanded ratio is 6:12. For 6 pints, the measurement is 12 cups. This problem can also be set up as one set of fractions to cancel out units. It begins with the given information and cancels out matching units on top and bottom to yield the answer. Consider the following expression:

$$\frac{3\ quarts}{1} \times \frac{2\ pints}{1\ quart} \times \frac{2\ cups}{1\ pint}$$

It's set up so that units on the top and bottom cancel each other out:

$$\frac{3\ \cancel{quarts}}{1} \times \frac{2\ \cancel{pints}}{1\ \cancel{quart}} \times \frac{2\ cups}{1\ \cancel{pint}}$$

The numbers can be calculated as $3 \times 3 \times 2$ on the top and 1 on the bottom. It still yields an answer of 12 cups.

This process of setting up fractions and canceling out matching units can be used to convert between standard and metric systems. A few common equivalent conversions are 2.54 cm = 1 inch, 3.28 feet = 1 meter, and 2.205 pounds = 1 kilogram. Writing these as fractions allows them to be used in conversions. For the fill-in-the-blank problem 5 meters = ____ feet, an expression using conversions starts with the expression $\frac{5\ meters}{1} \times \frac{3.28\ feet}{1\ meter}$, where the units of meters will cancel each other out, and the final unit is feet. Calculating the numbers yields 16.4 feet. This problem only required two fractions. Others may require longer expressions, but the underlying rule stays the same. When there's a unit on the top of the fraction that's the same as the unit on the bottom, then they cancel each other out. Using this logic and the conversions given above, many units can be converted between and within the different systems.

The conversion between Fahrenheit and Celsius is found in a formula: $°C = (°F - 32) \times \frac{5}{9}$. For example, to convert 78°F to Celsius, the given temperature would be entered into the formula: $°C = (78 - 32) \times \frac{5}{9}$. Solving the equation, the temperature comes out to be 25.56°C. To convert in the other direction, the formula becomes: $°F = °C \times \frac{9}{5} + 32$. Remember the order of operations when calculating these conversions.

Simple Geometry Problems

Area
Area is the two-dimensional space covered by an object. These problems may include the area of a rectangle, a yard, or a wall to be painted. Finding the area may be a simple formula, or it may require multiple formulas to be used together. The units for area are square units, such as square meters, square inches, and square miles. Given a square with side length *s*, the formula for its area is $A = s^2$.

Some other formulas for common shapes are shown below.

Shape	Formula	Graphic
Rectangle	$Area = length \times width$	
Triangle	$Area = \dfrac{1}{2} \times base \times height$	
Circle	$Area = \pi \times radius^2$	

The following formula, not as widely used as those shown above, but very important, is the area of a trapezoid:

Area of a Trapezoid

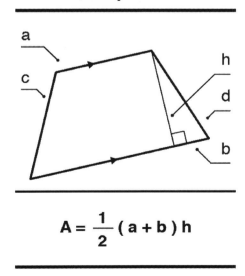

$$A = \frac{1}{2}(a + b)h$$

To find the area of the shapes above, use the given dimensions of the shape in the formula. Complex shapes might require more than one formula. To find the area of the figure below, break the figure into two shapes. The rectangle has dimensions 11 cm by 6 cm. The triangle has dimensions 3 cm by 6 cm. Plug the dimensions into the rectangle formula: $A = 11 \times 6$. Multiplication yields an area of 66 cm². The triangle area can be found using the formula $A = \frac{1}{2} \times 4 \times 6$. Multiplication yields an area of 12 cm². Add the areas of the two shapes to find the total area of the figure, which is 78 cm².

Instead of combining areas, some problems may require subtracting them, or finding the difference.

To find the area of the shaded region in the figure below, determine the area of the whole figure. Then the area of the circle can be subtracted from the whole.

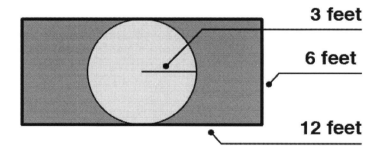

The following formula shows the area of the outside rectangle: $A = 12 \times 6 = 72 \ ft^2$. The area of the inside circle can be found by the following formula: $A = \pi r^2 = \pi(3^2) = 9\pi = 28.27 \ ft^2$. As the shaded area is outside the circle, the area for the circle can be subtracted from the area of the rectangle to yield an area of $43.73 \ ft^2$.

Perimeter
Perimeter is the distance around an object. The perimeter of an object can be found by adding the lengths of all sides. Perimeter may be used in problems dealing with lengths around objects such as

fences or borders. It may also be used in finding missing lengths or working backwards. If the perimeter is given, but a length is missing, use subtraction to find the missing length. Given a square with side length s, the formula for perimeter is $P = 4s$. Given a rectangle with length l and width w, the formula for perimeter is $P = 2l + 2w$. The perimeter of a triangle is found by adding the three side lengths, and the perimeter of a trapezoid is found by adding the four side lengths. The units for perimeter are always the original units of length, such as meters, inches, miles, etc. When discussing a circle, the distance around the object is referred to as its circumference, not perimeter. The formula for circumference of a circle is $C = 2\pi r$, where r represents the radius of the circle. This formula can also be written as $C = d\mu$, where d represents the diameter of the circle.

Volume

Volume is three-dimensional and describes the amount of space that an object occupies, but it's different from area because it has three dimensions instead of two. The units for volume are cubic units, such as cubic meters, cubic inches, and cubic miles. Volume can be found by using formulas for common objects such as cylinders and boxes.

The following chart shows a diagram and formula for the volume of two objects.

Shape	Formula	Diagram
Rectangular Prism (box)	$V = length \times width \times height$	
Cylinder	$V = \pi \times radius^2 \times height$	

Volume formulas of these two objects are derived by finding the area of the bottom two-dimensional shape, such as the circle or rectangle, and then multiplying times the height of the three-dimensional shape. Other volume formulas include the volume of a cube with side length s: $V = s^3$; the volume of a sphere with radius r. $V = \frac{4}{3}\pi r^3$; and the volume of a cone with radius r and height h. $V = \frac{1}{3}\pi r^2 h$.

If a soda can has a height of 5 inches and a radius on the top of 1.5 inches, the volume can be found using one of the given formulas. A soda can is a cylinder. Knowing the given dimensions, the formula can be completed as follows: $V = \pi (radius)^2 \times height = \pi (1.5)^2 \times 5 = 35.325\ inches^3$. Notice that the units for volume are inches cubed because it refers to the number of cubic inches required to fill the can.

Solving for Missing Values in Triangles, Circles, and Other Figures

Solving for missing values in shapes requires knowledge of the shape and its characteristics. For example, a triangle has three sides and three angles that add up to 180 degrees. If two angle measurements are given, the third can be calculated. For the triangle below, the one given angle has a measure of 55 degrees. The missing angle is x. The third angle is labeled with a square, which indicates a measure of 90 degrees. Because all angles must sum to 180 degrees, the following equation can be used to find the missing x-value: $55 + 90 + x = 180$. Adding the two given angles and subtracting the total from 180, the missing angle is found to be 35 degrees.

A similar problem can be solved with circles. If the radius is given, but the circumference is unknown, it can be calculated based on the formula $C = 2\pi r$. This example can be used in the figure below. The radius can be substituted for r in the formula. Then the circumference can be found as $C = 2\pi \times 8 = 16\pi = 50.24\ cm$.

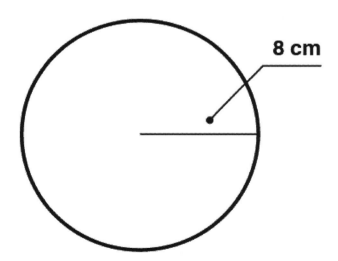

Other figures that may have missing values could be the length of a square, given the area, or the perimeter of a rectangle, given the length and width. All of the missing values can be found by first identifying all the characteristics that are known about the shape, then looking for ways to connect the missing value to the given information.

Distribution of a Quantity into its Fractional Parts

Fractions are ratios of whole numbers and their negatives. Fractions represent parts of wholes, whether they be pies, or money, or work. The number on top, or numerator, represents the part, and the bottom number, or denominator, represents the whole. The number $\frac{1}{2}$ represents half of a whole. Other ways to represent one-half are $\frac{2}{4}, \frac{3}{6}$, and $\frac{5}{10}$. These are fractions not written in simplest form, but the numerators are all halves of the denominators. The fraction $\frac{1}{4}$ represents 1 part to a whole of 4 parts. This can be seen by the quarter's value in relation to the dollar. One quarter is $\frac{1}{4}$ of a dollar. In the same way, 2 quarters make up $\frac{1}{2}$ of a dollar, so 2 fractions of $\frac{1}{4}$ make up a fraction of $\frac{1}{2}$. Three quarters make up three-fourths of a dollar. The three fractions of $\frac{1}{4} + \frac{1}{4} + \frac{1}{4}$ are equal to $\frac{3}{4}$ of a whole. This illustration can be seen using the bars below divided into one whole, then two halves, then three sections of one-third, then four sections of one-fourth. Based on the size of the fraction, different numbers of each fraction are needed to make up a whole.

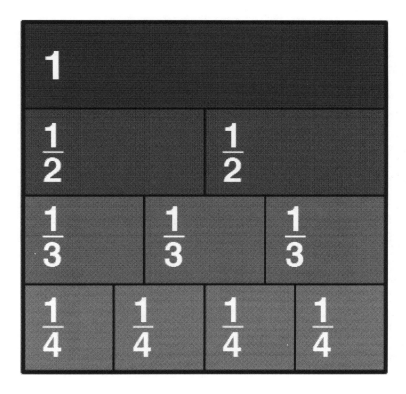

A *unit fraction* is a fraction where the numerator has a value of one. The fractions one-half, one-third, one-seventh, and one-tenth are all examples of unit fractions. Non-examples of unit fractions include three-fourths, four-fifths, and seven-twelfths. The value of unit fractions changes as the denominator changes because the numerator is always one. The unit fraction one-half requires two parts to make a whole. The unit fraction one-third requires three parts to make a whole. In the same way, if the unit fraction changes to one-thirteenth, then the number of parts required to make a whole becomes thirteen. An illustration of this is seen in the figure below. As the denominator increases, the size of the parts for each fraction decreases. As the bar goes from one-fourth to one-fifth, the size of the bars decreases, but the size of the denominator increases to five. This pattern continues down the diagram, and as the bars, or value of the fraction, get smaller, the denominator gets larger.

Using the Same Whole When Comparing Fractions

Comparing fractions requires the use of a common denominator. The necessity of this can be seen by the two pies below. The first pie has a shaded value of $\frac{2}{10}$ because two pieces are shaded out of the whole of ten pieces. The second pie has a shaded value of $\frac{2}{7}$ because two pieces are shaded out of a whole of seven pieces. These two fractions, two-tenths and two-sevenths, have the same numerator, and so a misconception may be that they are equal. By looking at the shaded region in each pie, it is apparent that the fractions are not equal. The numerators are the same, but the denominators are not. Two parts of a whole are not equivalent unless the whole is broken into the same number of parts. To compare the shaded regions, the denominators seven and ten must be made equal. The lowest number that the two denominators will both divide evenly into is 70, which is the lowest common denominator. Then the numerators must be converted by multiplying by the opposite denominator. These operations result in the two fractions $\frac{14}{70}$ and $\frac{20}{70}$. Now that these two have the same denominator, the conclusion can be made that $\frac{2}{7}$ represents a larger portion of the pie, as seen in the figure below.

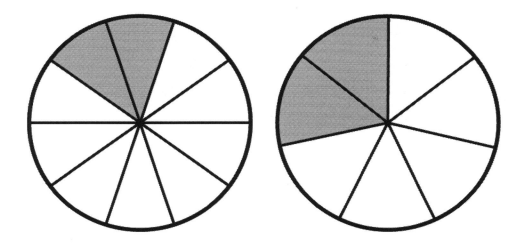

Practice Questions

1. What is $\frac{12}{60}$ converted to a percentage?
    a. 0.20
    b. 20%
    c. 25%
    d. 12%

2. Which of the following is the correct decimal form of the fraction $\frac{14}{33}$ rounded to the nearest hundredth place?
    a. 0.420
    b. 0.42
    c. 0.424
    d. 0.140

3. Which of the following represents the correct sum of $\frac{14}{15}$ and $\frac{2}{5}$?
    a. $\frac{20}{15}$

    b. $\frac{4}{3}$

    c. $\frac{16}{20}$

    d. $\frac{4}{5}$

4. What is the product of $\frac{5}{14}$ and $\frac{7}{20}$?
    a. $\frac{1}{8}$

    b. $\frac{35}{280}$

    c. $\frac{12}{34}$

    d. $\frac{1}{2}$

5. What is the result of dividing 24 by $\frac{8}{5}$?
    a. $\frac{5}{3}$

    b. $\frac{3}{5}$

    c. $\frac{120}{8}$

    d. 15

6. Subtract $\frac{5}{14}$ from $\frac{5}{24}$. Which of the following is the correct result?

   a. $\frac{25}{168}$

   b. 0

   c. $-\frac{25}{168}$

   d. $\frac{1}{10}$

7. Which of the following is a correct mathematical statement?

   a. $\frac{1}{3} < -\frac{4}{3}$

   b. $-\frac{1}{3} > \frac{4}{3}$

   c. $\frac{1}{3} > -\frac{4}{3}$

   d. $-\frac{1}{3} \geq \frac{4}{3}$

8. Which of the following is incorrect?

   a. $-\frac{1}{5} < \frac{4}{5}$

   b. $\frac{4}{5} > -\frac{1}{5}$

   c. $-\frac{1}{5} > \frac{4}{5}$

   d. $\frac{1}{5} > -\frac{4}{5}$

9. In a neighborhood, 15 out of 80 of the households have children under the age of 18. What percentage of the households have children?

   a. 0.1875%
   b. 18.75%
   c. 1.875%
   d. 15%

10. Gina took an algebra test last Friday. There were 35 questions, and she answered 60% of them correctly. How many correct answers did she have?

   a. 35
   b. 20
   c. 21
   d. 25

11. Paul took a written driving test, and he got 12 of the questions correct. If he answered 75% of the total questions correctly, how many problems were there in the test?

    a. 25

    b. 16

    c. 20

    d. 18

12. If a car is purchased for $15,395 with a 7.25% sales tax, how much is the total price?

    a. $15,395.07

    b. $16,511.14

    c. $16,411.13

    d. $15,402

13. A car manufacturer usually makes 15,412 SUVs, 25,815 station wagons, 50,412 sedans, 8,123 trucks, and 18,312 hybrids a month. About how many cars are manufactured each month?

    a. 120,000

    b. 200,000

    c. 300,000

    d. 12,000

14. Each year, a family goes to the grocery store every week and spends $105. About how much does the family spend annually on groceries?

    a. $10,000

    b. $50,000

    c. $500

    d. $5,000

15. Bindee is having a barbeque on Sunday and needs 12 packets of ketchup for every 5 guests. If 60 guests are coming, how many packets of ketchup should she buy?

    a. 100

    b. 12

    c. 144

    d. 60

16. A grocery store sold 48 bags of apples in one day, and 9 of the bags contained Granny Smith apples. The rest contained Red Delicious apples. What is the ratio of bags of Granny Smith to bags of Red Delicious that were sold?

    a. 48:9

    b. 39:9

    c. 9:48

    d. 9:39

17. If Oscar's bank account totaled $4,000 in March and $4,900 in June, what was the rate of change in his bank account total over those three months?

    a. $900 a month

    b. $300 a month

    c. $4,900 a month

    d. $100 a month

18. What is the resultant matrix when addition is performed?

$$\begin{bmatrix} 1 & -5 \\ 4 & 2 \end{bmatrix} + \begin{bmatrix} 3 & 2 \\ -2 & 1 \end{bmatrix} = \begin{bmatrix} & \\ & \end{bmatrix}$$

a. $\begin{bmatrix} 3 & -2 \\ 5 & 0 \end{bmatrix}$

b. $\begin{bmatrix} 4 & 3 \\ 2 & 3 \end{bmatrix}$

c. $\begin{bmatrix} 4 & -3 \\ 2 & 3 \end{bmatrix}$

d. $\begin{bmatrix} 3 & -3 \\ -3 & 3 \end{bmatrix}$

19. What is the area of the shaded region?

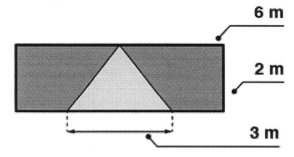

6 m

2 m

3 m

a. 9 m²
b. 12 m²
c. 6 m²
d. 8 m²

20. What is the volume of the cylinder below?

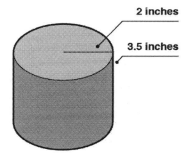

2 inches

3.5 inches

a. 18.84 in³
b. 45.00 in³
c. 70.43 in³
d. 43.96 in³

21. Which of the following is equivalent to $16^{\frac{1}{4}}16^{\frac{1}{2}}$?

    a. 8

    b. 16

    c. 4

    d. 4,096

22. What is the area of the following figure?

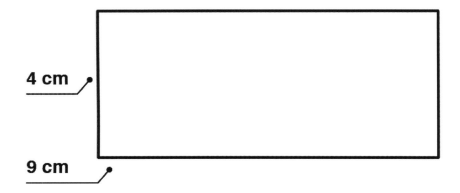

    a. 26 cm

    b. 36 cm

    c. 13 cm^2

    d. 36 cm^2

Answer Explanations

1. B: The fraction $\frac{12}{60}$ can be reduced to $\frac{1}{5}$, in lowest terms. First, it must be converted to a decimal. Dividing 1 by 5 results in 0.2. Then, to convert to a percentage, move the decimal point two units to the right and add the percentage symbol. The result is 20%.

2. B: If a calculator is used, divide 33 into 14 and keep two decimal places. If a calculator is not used, multiply both the numerator and denominator times 3. This results in the fraction $\frac{42}{99}$, and hence a decimal of 0.42.

3. B: Common denominators must be used. The LCD is 15, and $\frac{2}{5} = \frac{6}{15}$. Therefore, $\frac{14}{15} + \frac{6}{15} = \frac{20}{15}$, and in lowest terms the answer is $\frac{4}{3}$. A common factor of 5 was divided out of both the numerator and denominator.

4. A: A product is found by multiplication. Multiplying two fractions together is easier when common factors are cancelled first to avoid working with larger numbers. $\frac{5}{14} \times \frac{7}{20} = \frac{5}{2\times7} \times \frac{7}{5\times4} = \frac{1}{2} \times \frac{1}{4} = \frac{1}{8}$.

5. D: Division is completed by multiplying times the reciprocal. Therefore, $24 \div \frac{8}{5} = \frac{24}{1} \times \frac{5}{8} = \frac{3\times8}{1} \times \frac{5}{8} = \frac{15}{1} = 15$.

6. C: Common denominators must be used. The LCD is 168, so each fraction must be converted to have 168 as the denominator. $\frac{5}{24} - \frac{5}{14} = \frac{5}{24} \times \frac{7}{7} - \frac{5}{14} \times \frac{12}{12} = \frac{35}{168} - \frac{60}{168} = -\frac{25}{168}$.

7. C: The correct mathematical statement is the one in which the number to the left on the number line is less than the number to the right on the number line. It is written in Choice *C* that $\frac{1}{3} > -\frac{4}{3}$, which is the same as $-\frac{4}{3} < \frac{1}{3}$, a correct statement.

8. C: $-\frac{1}{5} > \frac{4}{5}$ is incorrect. The expression on the left is negative, which means that it is smaller than the expression on the right. As it is written, the inequality states that the expression on the left is greater than the expression on the right, which is not true.

9. B: First, the information is translated into the ratio $\frac{15}{80}$. To find the percentage, translate this fraction into a decimal by dividing 15 by 80. The corresponding decimal is 0.1875. Move the decimal point two units to the right to obtain the percentage 18.75%.

10. C: Gina answered 60% of 35 questions correctly; 60% can be expressed as the decimal 0.60. Therefore, she answered $0.60 \times 35 = 21$ questions correctly.

11. B: The unknown quantity is the number of total questions on the test. Let x be equal to this unknown quantity. Therefore, $0.75x = 12$. Divide both sides by 0.75 to obtain $x = 16$.

12. B: If sales tax is 7.25%, the price of the car must be multiplied times 1.0725 to account for the additional sales tax. Therefore, $15,395 \times 1.0725 = 16,511.1375$. This amount is rounded to the nearest cent, which is $16,511.14.

13. A: Rounding can be used to find the best approximation. All of the values can be rounded to the nearest thousand. 15,412 SUVs can be rounded to 15,000. 25,815 station wagons can be rounded to

26,000. 50,412 sedans can be rounded to 50,000. 8,123 trucks can be rounded to 8,000. Finally, 18,312 hybrids can be rounded to 18,000. The sum of the rounded values is 117,000, which is closest to 120,000.

14. D: There are 52 weeks in a year, and if the family spends $105 each week, that amount is close to $100. A good approximation is $100 a week for 50 weeks, which is found through the product $50 \times 100 = \$5,000$.

15. C: This problem involves ratios and percentages. If 12 packets are needed for every 5 people, this statement is equivalent to the ratio $\frac{12}{5}$. The unknown amount x is the number of ketchup packets needed for 60 people. The proportion $\frac{12}{5} = \frac{x}{60}$ must be solved. Cross-multiply to obtain $12 \times 60 = 5x$. Therefore, $720 = 5x$. Divide each side by 5 to obtain $x = 144$.

16. D: There were 48 total bags of apples sold. If 9 bags were Granny Smith and the rest were Red Delicious, then $48 - 9 = 39$ bags were Red Delicious. Therefore, the ratio of Granny Smith to Red Delicious is 9:39.

17. B: The average rate of change is found by calculating the difference in dollars over the elapsed time. Therefore, the rate of change is equal to $4,900-$4,000÷3 months, which is equal to $900÷3 or $300 a month.

18. C: The correct answer is Choice *C* because matrices are added by adding the corresponding numbers in the two given matrices. For matrices to be added, they must have the same number of rows and columns. These two matrices have two rows and two columns. The first row, first column numbers are 1 and 3, and adding them together yields a total of 4. The second row, first column has numbers 4 and –2, which yields a sum of 2. The first row, second column has –5 and 2, which yields a sum of –3. The second row, second column have 2 and 1, which yield a sum of 3. The resulting matrix after addition is: $\begin{bmatrix} 4 & -3 \\ 2 & 3 \end{bmatrix}$.

19. A: The area of the shaded region is calculated in a few steps. First, the area of the rectangle is found using the formula $A = length \times width = 6 \times 2 = 12$. Second, the area of the triangle is found using the formula: $A = \frac{1}{2} \times base \times height = \frac{1}{2} \times 3 \times 2 = 3$. The last step is to take the rectangle area and subtract the triangle area. The area of the shaded region is $A = 12 - 3 = 9m^2$.

20. D: The volume for a cylinder is found by using the formula: $V = \pi r^2 h = \pi(2^2) \times 3.5 = 43.96 in^3$.

21. A: The corresponding expression written using common denominators of the exponents is $16^{\frac{1}{4}}16^{\frac{2}{4}}$, and then the expression is written as $(16 \times 16^2)^{\frac{1}{4}}$. This can be written in radical notation as $\sqrt[4]{16^3} = \sqrt[4]{4,096} = 8$.

22. D: The area for a rectangle is found by multiplying the length by the width. The area is also measured in square units, so the correct answer is Choice *D*. The answer of 26 is the perimeter. The answer of 13 is found by adding the two dimensions instead of multiplying.

College-Level Math

Algebraic Operations

Algebraic Expressions

An *algebraic expression* is a mathematical phrase that may contain numbers, variables, and mathematical operations. An expression represents a single quantity. For example, $3x + 2$ is an algebraic expression.

An *algebraic equation* is a mathematical sentence with two expressions that are equal to each other. That is, an equation must contain an equals sign, as in $3x + 2 = 17$. This statement says that the value of the expression on the left side of the equals sign is equivalent to the value of the expression on the right side. In an expression, there are not two sides because there is no equals sign. The equals sign ($=$) is the difference between an expression and an equation.

To distinguish an expression from an equation, just look for the equals sign.

Example: Determine whether each of these is an expression or an equation.

a. $16 + 4x = 9x - 7$ Solution: Equation

b. $-27x - 42 + 19y$ Solution: Expression

c. $4 = x + 3$ Solution: Equation

Adding and Subtracting Linear Algebraic Expressions
To add and subtract linear algebra expressions, you must combine like terms. *Like terms* are described as those terms that have the same variable with the same exponent. In the following example, the x-terms can be added because the variable is the same and the exponent on the variable of one is also the same. These terms add to be $9x$. The other like terms are called *constants* because they have no variable component. These terms will add to be nine.

Example: Add $(3x - 5) + (6x + 14)$

                    $3x - 5 + 6x + 14$ Rewrite without parentheses

                    $3x + 6x - 5 + 14$ Commutative property of addition

                    $9x + 9$ Combine like terms

When subtracting linear expressions, be careful to add the opposite when combining like terms. Do this by distributing -1, which is multiplying each term inside the second parenthesis by negative one. Remember that distributing -1 changes the sign of each term.

Example: Subtract $(17x + 3) - (27x - 8)$

                    $17x + 3 - 27x + 8$ Distributive Property

                    $17x - 27x + 3 + 8$ Commutative property of addition

                    $-10x + 11$ Combine like terms

Example: Simplify by adding or subtracting:

$$(6m + 28z - 9) + (14m + 13) - (-4z + 8m + 12)$$

$6m + 28z - 9 + 14m + 13 + 4z - 8m - 12$	Distributive Property
$6m + 14m - 8m + 28z + 4z - 9 + 13 - 12$	Commutative Property of Addition
$12m + 32z - 8$	Combine like terms

Using the Distributive Property to Generate Equivalent Linear Algebraic Expressions
The Distributive Property: $a(b + c) = ab + ac$

The *distributive property* is a way of taking a factor and multiplying it through a given expression in parentheses. Each term inside the parentheses is multiplied by the outside factor, eliminating the parentheses. The following example shows how to distribute the number 3 to all the terms inside the parentheses.

Example: Use the distributive property to write an equivalent algebraic expression:

$$3(2x + 7y + 6)$$

$3(2x) + 3(7y) + 3(6)$	Distributive property
$6x + 21y + 18$	Simplify

Because $a - b$ can be written $a + (-b)$, the distributive property can be applied in the example below.

Example:　　Use the distributive property to write an equivalent algebraic expression.

$$7(5m - 8)$$

$7[5m + (-8)]$	Rewrite subtraction as addition of -8
$7(5m) + 7(-8)$	Distributive property
$35m - 56$	Simplify

In the following example, note that the factor of 2 is written to the right of the parentheses but is still distributed as before.

Example:　　Use the distributive property to write an equivalent algebraic expression:

$$(3m + 4x - 10)2$$

$(3m)2 + (4x)2 + (-10)2$	Distributive property
$6m + 8x - 20$	Simplify

Example:　　$-(-2m + 6x)$

In this example, the negative sign in front of the parentheses can be interpreted as $-1(-2m + 6x)$

$$-1(-2m + 6x)$$

$$-1(-2m) + (-1)(6x)$$ Distributive property

$$2m - 6x$$ Simplify

Evaluating Simple Algebraic Expressions for Given Values of Variables

To evaluate an algebra expression for a given value of a variable, replace the variable with the given value. Then perform the given operations to simplify the expression.

Example: Evaluate $12 + x$ for $x = 9$

$12 + (9)$ Replace x with the value of 9 as given in the problem. *It is a good idea to always use parentheses when substituting this value. This will be particularly important in the following examples.*

21   Add

Now see that when x is 9, the value of the given expression is 21.

Example: Evaluate $4x + 7$ for $x = 3$

$4(3) + 7$ Replace the x in the expression with 3

$12 + 7$ Multiply (remember order of operations)

19   Add

Therefore, when x is 3, the value of the given expression is 19.

Example: Evaluate $-7m - 3r - 18$ for $m = 2$ and $r = -1$

$-7(2) - 3(-1) - 18$ Replace m with 2 and r with -1

$-14 + 3 - 18$ Multiply

-29 Add

So, when m is 2 and r is -1, the value of the given expression is -29.

Using Mathematical Terms to Identify Parts of Expressions and Describe Expressions

A *variable* is a symbol used to represent a number. Letters, like x, y, and z are often used as variables in algebra.

A *constant* is a number that cannot change its value. For example, 18 is a constant.   3

A *term* is a constant, variable, or the product of constants and variables. In an expression, terms are separated by + and − signs. Examples of terms are $24x$, −32, and $15xyz$.

Like terms are terms that contain the same variables. For example, $6z$ and $-8z$ are like terms, and $9xy$ and $17xy$ are like terms. Constants, like 23 and 51, are like terms as well.

A *factor* is something that is multiplied by something else. A factor may be a constant, a variable, or a sum of constants or variables.

A *coefficient* is the numerical factor in a term that has a variable. In the term 16x, the coefficient is 16.

Example: Given the expression, $6x - 12y + 18$, answer the following questions.

- How many terms are in the expression?
- Solution: 3
- Name the terms.
- Solution: 6x, −12y, and 18   (Notice that the minus sign preceding the 12 is interpreted to represent negative 12)
- Name the factors.
- Solution: 6, x, −12, y
- What are the coefficients in this expression?
- Solution: 6 and −12
- What is the constant in this expression?
- Solution: 18

Simplifying Rational Algebraic Expressions

When given a problem, it is necessary to determine the best form of an expression or equation to use, given the context. Usually this involves some algebraic manipulation. If an equation is given, the simplest form of the equation is best. Simplifying involves using the distributive property, collecting like terms, etc. If an equation is needed to be solved, properties involving performing the same operation on both sides of the equation must be used. For instance, if a number is added to one side of the equals sign, it must be added to the other side as well. This maintains a true equation.

If an expression is given, simplifying can only involve properties allowing to rewrite the expression as an equivalent form. If there is no equals sign, mathematical operations cannot be performed on the expression, unless it is a rational expression. A *rational expression* can be written in the form of a fraction, in which the numerator and denominator are both polynomials and the denominator is not equal to zero. Rational expressions can always be multiplied times a form of 1. For example, consider the following rational expression involving radicals: $\frac{2}{\sqrt{2}}$. It is incorrect to write a fraction with a root in the denominator, and therefore the expression must be rationalized. Multiply the fraction times $\frac{\sqrt{2}}{\sqrt{2}}$, a form of 1. This results in $\frac{2}{\sqrt{2}} \times \frac{\sqrt{2}}{\sqrt{2}} = \frac{2\sqrt{2}}{\sqrt{4}} = \frac{2\sqrt{2}}{2} = \sqrt{2}$, which is the most suitable form of the expression.

Creating an Equivalent Form of an Algebraic Expression
Two algebraic expressions are equivalent if, even though they look different, they represent the same expression. Therefore, plugging in the same values into the variables in each expression will result in the same result in both expressions. To obtain an equivalent form of an algebraic expression, laws of algebra must be followed. For instance, addition and multiplication are both commutative and associative. Therefore, terms in an algebraic expression can be added in any order and multiplied in any order. For instance, $4x + 2y$ is equivalent to $2y + 4x$ and $y \times 2 + x \times 4$. Also, the distributive law allows a number to be distributed throughout parentheses, as in the following: $a(b + c) = ab + ac$. The two expressions on both sides of the equals sign are equivalent. Also, collecting like terms is important when working with equivalent forms. The simplest version of an expression is always the one easiest to work with, so all like terms (those with the same variables raised to the same powers) must be combined.

Note that an expression is not an equation, and therefore expressions cannot be multiplied times numbers, divided by numbers, or have numbers added to them or subtracted from them and still have equivalent expressions. These processes can only happen in equations when the same step is performed on both sides of the equals sign.

Factoring

A factorization of an algebraic expression can be found. Throughout the process, a more complicated expression can be decomposed into products of simpler expressions. To factor a polynomial, first determine if there is a greatest common factor. If there is, factor it out. For example, $2x^2 + 8x$ has a greatest common factor of $2x$ and can be written as $2x(x + 4)$. Once the greatest common monomial factor is factored out, if applicable, count the number of terms in the polynomial. If there are two terms, is it a difference of squares, a sum of cubes, or a difference of cubes? If so, the following rules can be used:

$$a^2 - b^2 = (a + b)(a - b)$$

$$a^3 + b^3 = (a + b)(a^2 - ab + b^2)$$

$$a^3 - b^3 = (a + b)(a^2 + ab + b^2)$$

If there are three terms, and if the trinomial is a perfect square trinomial, it can be factored into the following:

$$a^2 + 2ab + b^2 = (a + b)^2$$

$$a^2 - 2ab + b^2 = (a - b)^2$$

If not, try factoring into a product of two binomials by trial and error into a form of $(x + p)(x + q)$. For example, to factor $x^2 + 6x + 8$, determine what two numbers have a product of 8 and a sum of 6. Those numbers are 4 and 2, so the trinomial factors into $(x + 2)(x + 4)$.

Finally, if there are four terms, try factoring by grouping. First, group terms together that have a common monomial factor. Then, factor out the common monomial factor from the first two terms. Next, look to see if a common factor can be factored out of the second set of two terms that results in a common binomial factor. Finally, factor out the common binomial factor of each expression, for example, $xy - x + 5y - 5 = x(y - 1) + 5(y - 1) = (y - 1)(x + 5)$.

After the expression is completely factored, check to see if the factorization is correct by multiplying to try to obtain the original expression. Factorizations are helpful in solving equations that consist of a polynomial set equal to 0. If the product of two algebraic expressions equals 0, then at least one of the factors is equal to 0. Therefore, factor the polynomial within the equation, set each factor equal to 0, and solve. For example, $x^2 + 7x - 18 = 0$ can be solved by factoring into $(x + 9)(x - 2) = 0$. Set each factor equal to 0, and solve to obtain $x = -9$ and $x = 2$.

Expanding Polynomials

A *polynomial* is a mathematical expression containing the sum and difference of one or more terms that are constants multiplied times variables raised to positive powers. A polynomial is considered expanded when there are no variables contained within parentheses, the distributive property has been carried out for any terms that were within parentheses, and like terms have been collected.

Recall that the *distributive property* is a way of taking a factor and multiplying it through a given expression in parentheses. Each term inside the parentheses is multiplied by the outside factor, eliminating the parentheses. In simple terms, the distributive property is: $a(b + c) = ab + ac$.

To exemplify how to use the distributive property and expand a polynomial, consider the equation $3(x + 2) - 5x = 4x + 1$. Use the distributive property to clear the parentheses. Therefore, multiply each term inside the parentheses by 3. This step results in $3x + 6 - 5x = 4x + 1$. Next, collect like terms on the left-hand side. *Like terms* are terms with the same variable or variables raised to the same exponent(s). Only like terms can be combined through addition or subtraction. After collecting like terms, the equation is $-2x + 6 = 4x + 1$. Finally, apply the addition and multiplication principles. Add $2x$ to both sides to obtain $6 = 6x + 1$. Then, subtract 1 from both sides to obtain $5 = 6x$. Finally, divide both sides by 6 to obtain the solution $\frac{5}{6} = x$.

Manipulating Roots and Exponents

Numbers can also be written using exponents. The number 7,000 can be written as $7 \times 1,000$ because 7 is in the thousands place. It can also be written as 7×10^3 because $1,000 = 10^3$. Another number that can use this notation is 500. It can be written as 5×100, or 5×10^2, because $100 = 10^2$. The number 30 can be written as 3×10, or 3×10^1, because $10 = 10^1$. Notice that each one of the exponents of 10 is equal to the number of zeros in the number. Seven is in the thousands place, with three zeros, and the exponent on ten is 3. The five is in the hundreds place, with two zeros, and the exponent on the ten is 2. A question may give the number 40,000 and ask for it to be rewritten using exponents of ten. Because the number has a four in the ten-thousands place and four zeros, it can be written using an exponent of four: 4×10^4.

The nth root of a is given as $\sqrt[n]{a}$, which is called a *radical*. Typical values for n are 2 and 3, which represent the square and cube roots. In this form, n represents an integer greater than or equal to 2, and a is a real number. If n is even, a must be nonnegative, and if n is odd, a can be any real number. This radical can be written in exponential form as $a^{\frac{1}{n}}$. Therefore, $\sqrt[4]{15}$ is the same as $15^{\frac{1}{4}}$ and $\sqrt[3]{-5}$ is the same as $(-5)^{\frac{1}{3}}$.

In a similar fashion, the nth root of a can be raised to a power m, which is written as $\left(\sqrt[n]{a}\right)^m$. This expression is the same as $\sqrt[n]{a^m}$. For example, $\sqrt[2]{4^3} = \sqrt[2]{64} = 8 = \left(\sqrt[2]{4}\right)^3 = 2^3$. Because $\sqrt[n]{a} = a^{\frac{1}{n}}$, both sides can be raised to an exponent of m, resulting in $\left(\sqrt[n]{a}\right)^m = \sqrt[n]{a^m} = a^{\frac{m}{n}}$. This rule allows:

$$\sqrt[2]{4^3} = \left(\sqrt[2]{4}\right)^3 = 4^{\frac{3}{2}} = (2^2)^{\frac{3}{2}} = 2^{\frac{6}{2}} = 2^3 = 8$$

Negative exponents can also be incorporated into these rules. Any time an exponent is negative, the base expression must be flipped to the other side of the fraction bar and rewritten with a positive exponent. For instance, $2^{-3} = \frac{1}{2^3} = \frac{1}{8}$. Therefore, two more relationships between radical and exponential expressions are $a^{-\frac{1}{n}} = \frac{1}{\sqrt[n]{a}}$ and:

$$a^{-\frac{m}{n}} = \frac{1}{\sqrt[n]{a^m}} = \frac{1}{\left(\sqrt[n]{a}\right)^m}$$

Thus, $8^{-3} = \frac{1}{\sqrt[3]{8}} = \frac{1}{2}$.

All of these relationships are very useful when simplifying complicated radical and exponential expressions. If an expression contains both forms, use one of these rules to change the expression to contain either all radicals or all exponential expressions. This process makes the entire expression much easier to work with, especially if the expressions are contained within equations.

Consider the following example: $\sqrt{x} \times \sqrt[4]{x}$. It is written in radical form; however, it can be simplified into one radical by using exponential expressions first. The expression can be written as $x^{\frac{1}{2}} \times x^{\frac{1}{4}}$. It can be combined into one base by adding the exponents as: $x^{\frac{1}{2}+\frac{1}{4}} = x^{\frac{3}{4}}$. Writing this back in radical form, the result is $\sqrt[4]{x^3}$.

Creating Equivalent Expressions Involving Rational Exponents and Radicals

Writing radical expressions into equivalent forms involving rational exponents can help in simplifying complex radical expressions. The rule that helps this conversion is $\sqrt[n]{x^m} = x^{\frac{m}{n}}$. If $m = 1$, the rule is simply $\sqrt[n]{x} = x^{\frac{1}{n}}$. For instance, consider the following expression: $\sqrt[4]{x} \sqrt[2]{y}$. It can be written as one radical expression, but first it needs to be converted to an equivalent expression using rational expressions. The equivalent expression is $x^{\frac{1}{4}} y^{\frac{1}{2}}$. The goal is to have one radical, which means one index n, so a common denominator of the exponents must be found. The common denominator is 4, so an equivalent expression is $x^{\frac{1}{4}} y^{\frac{2}{4}}$. The exponential rule $a^m b^m = (ab)^m$ can be used to, in a sense, factor out a $\frac{1}{4}$ out of both exponents. This process results in the expression $(xy^2)^{\frac{1}{4}}$, and its equivalent radical form is $\sqrt[4]{xy^2}$. Converting to rational exponents has allowed the entire expression to be written as one radical.

Another type of problem could involve going in the opposite direction: starting with rational exponents and using an equivalent radical form to simplify the expression. For instance, $32^{\frac{1}{5}}$ might not seem obviously equal to 2. However, putting it in its equivalent radical form $\sqrt[5]{32}$ shows that it is equivalent to the fifth root of 32, which is 2.

Solutions of Equations and Inequalities

The Solution of Linear and Quadratic Equations and Inequalities

Multistep one-variable equations involve the use of one variable in an equation with many operations. For example, the equation $2x + 4 = 10$ involves one variable, x, and multiple steps to solve for the value of x. The first step is to move the four to the opposite side of the equation by subtracting 4. The next step is to divide by 2. The final answer yields a value of 3 for the variable x. The steps for this process are shown below.

$$2x + 4 = 10$$

$$-4 \quad -4 \qquad\qquad \text{Subtract 4 on both sides}$$

$$2x = 6$$

$$\div 2 \quad \div 2 \qquad\qquad \text{Divide by 2 on both sides}$$

$$x = 3$$

When the result is found, the value of the variable must be interpreted. For this problem, a value of 3 can be understood as the amount that can be doubled and then increased by 4 to yield a value of 10.

Inequalities can also be interpreted in much the same way. The following inequality can be solved to find the value of b. $\frac{b}{7} - 8 \geq 7$. This inequality models the amount of money a group of friends earned for cleaning up a neighbor's yard, *b*. There were 7 friends, so the money had to be split seven times. Then $8 was taken away from each friend to pay for materials they bought to help clean the yard. All these things needed to be less than or equal to seven for the friends to each receive at least $7. The first step is to add 8 to both sides of the inequality. Then the 7 can be multiplied on each side. The resulting inequality is $b \geq$ 105. Because the answer is not only an equals sign, the value for *b* is not a single number. In this problem, the answer communicates that the value of *b* must be greater than or equal to $105 in order for each friend to make at least $7 for their work. The number for *b*, what they are paid, can be more than 105 because that would mean they earned more money. They do not want it to be less than 105 because their profit will drop below $7 apiece.

Equation Systems

Simultaneous equations, otherwise known as a *system of equations*, can be solved in a variety of ways. If the system consists of two linear equations, they can be solved by graphing, substitution, or elimination.

When graphing, the solution of a system of equations is the point of intersection. If the two lines are parallel, they will never intersect, and there is no solution. If the two lines are the same, there are infinitely many solutions, and the solution set is equal to the entire line. Here are the three cases:

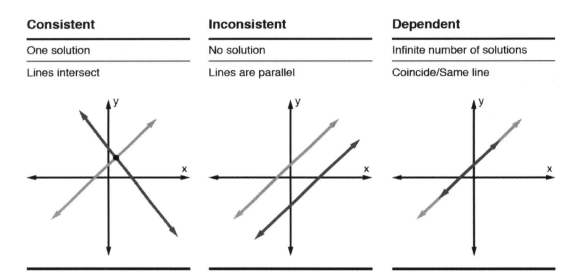

Consistent	**Inconsistent**	**Dependent**
One solution	No solution	Infinite number of solutions
Lines intersect	Lines are parallel	Coincide/Same line

There are two algebraic methods to finding solutions. The first is *substitution*. This is better suited when one of the equations is already solved for one variable, or it is easy to do so. Then this equation gets substituted into the other equation for that variable, resulting in an equation in one variable. Solve for the given variable and plug that value into one of the original equations to find the other variable. This last step is known as *back-substitution*.

Here is an example of solving a system with the substitution method:

$$y=x+1 \qquad 2y=3x$$

$$2y=3x$$
$$2(x+1)=3x$$
$$2x+2=3x$$
$$\underline{-2x \quad -2x}$$
$$2=x$$

$$y=x+1$$
$$y=2+1=3$$

Solution: (2,3)

The other method is known as *elimination*, or the *addition method*. This is better suited when the equations are in standard form: $Ax + By = C$. The goal in this method is to multiply one or both equations times numbers that result in opposite coefficients. Then add the equations together to obtain an equation in one variable. Solve for the given variable, and then take that value and back-substitute to obtain the other part of the ordered pair solution. Here is an example of elimination:

$$\begin{cases} -x + 5y = 8 \\ 3x + 7y = -2 \end{cases} \xrightarrow{\times 3} \begin{cases} -3x + 15y = 24 \\ 3x + 7y = -2 \end{cases}$$

$$-3x + 15y = 24$$
$$\underline{3x + 7y = -2}$$
$$22y = 22$$

$$\frac{22y}{22} = \frac{22}{22}$$

$$y = 1$$

Note that in order to check an answer when solving a system of equations, the solution must be checked in both original equations to show that it solves both equations.

<u>Systems of Linear Inequalities in Two Variables</u>

A *system of linear inequalities in two variables* consists of two inequalities in two variables, *x* and *y*. For example, the following is a system of linear inequalities in two variables:

$$\begin{cases} 4x + 2y < 1 \\ 2x - y \le 0 \end{cases}$$

The curly brace on the left side shows that the two inequalities are grouped together. A solution of a single inequality in two variables is an ordered pair that satisfies the inequality. For example, (1, 3) is a solution of the linear inequality $y \ge x + 1$ because when plugged in, it results in a true statement. The graph of an inequality in two variables consists of all ordered pairs that make the solution true. Therefore, the entire solution set of a single inequality contains many ordered pairs, and the set can be graphed by using a half plane. A *half plane* consists of the set of all points on one side of a line. If the inequality consists of > or <, the line is dashed because no solutions actually exist on the line shown. If the inequality consists of $\ge$ or $\le$, the line is solid and solutions are on the line shown. To graph a linear inequality, graph the corresponding equation found by replacing the inequality symbol with an equals sign. Then pick a test point that exists on either side of the line. If that point results in a true statement when plugged into the original inequality, shade in the side containing the test point. If it results in a false statement, shade in the opposite side.

Solving a system of linear inequalities must be done graphically. Follow the process as described above for both given inequalities. The solution set to the entire system is the region that is in common to every graph in the system. For example, here is the solution to the following system:

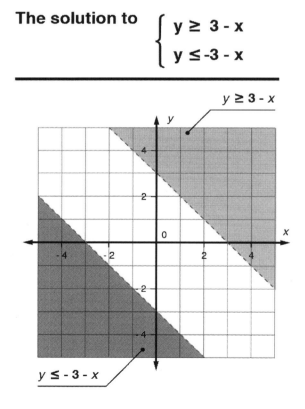

The solution to $\begin{cases} y \ge 3 - x \\ y \le -3 - x \end{cases}$

$y \ge 3 - x$

$y \le -3 - x$

Note that there is no region in common, so this system has no solution.

Systems of Two Linear Equations in Two Variables
An example of a *system of two linear equations in two variables* is the following:

$$2x + 5y = 8$$

$$5x + 48y = 9$$

A solution to a *system of two linear equations* is an ordered pair that satisfies both the equations in the system. A system can have one solution, no solution, or infinitely many solutions. The solution can be found through a graphing technique. The solution of a system of equations is actually equal to the point of intersection of both lines. If the lines intersect at one point, there is one solution and the system is said to be consistent. However, if the two lines are parallel, they will never intersect and there is no solution. In this case, the system is said to be inconsistent. Third, if the two lines are actually the same line, there are infinitely many solutions and the solution set is equal to the entire line. The lines are dependent. Here is a summary of the three cases:

Solving Systems by Graphing

Consistent	**Inconsistent**	**Dependent**
One solution	No solution	Infinite number of solutions
Lines intersect	*Lines are parallel*	*Coincide: same line*

Consider the following system of equations:

$$y + x = 3$$

$$y - x = 1$$

To find the solution graphically, graph both lines on the same *xy*-plane. Graph each line using either a table of ordered pairs, the *x*- and *y*-intercepts, or slope and the *y*-intercept. Then, locate the point of intersection.

The graph is shown here:

The System of Equations $\begin{cases} y + x = 3 \\ y - x = 1 \end{cases}$

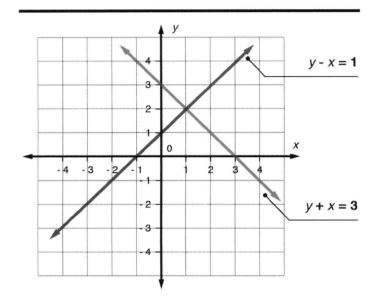

It can be seen that the point of intersection is the ordered pair (1, 2). This solution can be checked by plugging it back into both original equations to make sure it results in true statements. This process results in:

$$2 + 1 = 3$$

$$2 - 1 = 1$$

Both are true equations, so therefore the point of intersection is truly the solution.

The following system has no solution:

$$y = 4x + 1$$

$$y = 4x - 1$$

Both lines have the same slope and different y-intercepts, and therefore they are parallel. This means that they run alongside each other and never intersect.

Finally, the following solution has infinitely many solutions:

$$2x - 7y = 12$$

$$4x - 14y = 24$$

Note that the second equation is equal to the first equation times 2. Therefore, they are the same line. The solution set can be written in set notation as $\{(x, y)|2x - 7y = 12\}$, which represents the entire line.

Algebraically Solving Linear Equations or Inequalities in One Variable
A *linear equation in one variable* can be solved using the following steps:

1. Simplify the algebraic expressions on both sides of the equals sign by removing all parentheses, using the distributive property, and then collect all like terms.

2. Collect all variable terms on one side of the equals sign and all constant terms on the other side by adding the same quantity to both sides of the equals sign, or by subtracting the same quantity from both sides of the equals sign.

3. Isolate the variable by either dividing both sides of the equation by the same number, or by multiplying both sides by the same number.

4. Check the answer.

The only difference between solving linear inequalities versus equations is that when multiplying by a negative number or dividing by a negative number, the direction of the inequality symbol must be reversed.

If an equation contains multiple fractions, it might make sense to clear the equation of fractions first by multiplying all terms by the least common denominator. Also, if an equation contains several decimals, it might make sense to clear the decimals as well by multiplying times a factor of 10. If the equation has decimals in the hundredth place, multiply every term in the equation by 100.

Algebraically Solving Systems of Two Linear Equations in Two Variables
There are two algebraic methods to finding solutions. The first is substitution. This process is better suited for systems when one of the equations is already solved for one variable, or when solving for one variable is easy to do. The equation that is already solved for is substituted into the other equation for that variable, and this process results in a linear equation in one variable. This equation can be solved for the given variable, and then that solution can be plugged into one of the original equations, which can then be solved for the other variable. This last step is known as *back-substitution* and the end result is an ordered pair.

A system that is best suited for substitution is the following:

$$y = 4x + 2$$

$$2x + 3y = 9$$

The other method is known as *elimination*, or the *addition method*. This is better suited when the equations are in standard form $Ax + By = C$. The goal in this method is to multiply one or both equations times numbers that result in opposite coefficients. Then, add the equations together to obtain an equation in one variable. Solve for the given variable, then take that value and back-substitute to obtain the other part of the ordered pair solution.

A system that is best suited for elimination is the following:

$$2x + 3y = 8$$

$$4x - 2y = 10$$

Note that in order to check an answer when solving a system of equations, the solution must be checked in both original equations to show that it solves not only one of the equations, but both of them.

If throughout either solution procedure the process results in an untrue statement, there is no solution to the system. Finally, if throughout either solution procedure the process results in the variables dropping out, which gives a statement that is always true, there are infinitely many solutions.

Other Algebraic Equations

The graph of a linear equation is a line, and the graph of a quadratic equation is a parabola. Together, they form a system of a linear and quadratic equation. Here is an example of such a system:

$$\begin{cases} y = -2x + 3 \\ y = x^2 - 6x + 3 \end{cases}$$

Its solution consists of the points in which the two graphs intersect. Therefore, they can be solved graphically by physically locating those points, as in the following graphic:

The Graph of the System has Two Solutions: $\begin{cases} y = -2x + 3 \\ y = x^2 - 6x + 3 \end{cases}$

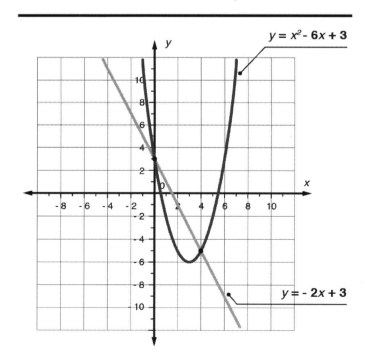

In this example, there are two points at which the graphs intersect, so there are two solutions. However, there could also be only one solution, as seen in the following example:

A System of Equations with a Single Solution

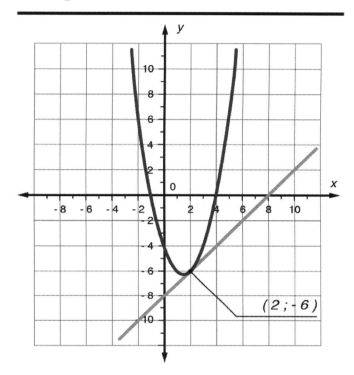

Third, it could be true that the graphs do not intersect, and in this case, there is no solution.

The solutions can also be found algebraically. In this case, solve for y in both equations and then set them equal to one another, as an equation in one variable, x. Then, put it in *standard form*, meaning move all terms to one side of the equals sign so that 0 is on the other side. This results in a quadratic equation that needs to be solved. It can be solved using factoring, completing the square, or by applying the quadratic formula. This results in either one solution (one point of intersection), two solutions (two points of intersection), or complex number solutions (no solution, no points of intersection). Then, substitute the x-values back into the linear equation to find the corresponding y-values. This results in the entire ordered pair solutions of the system.

The system above already has both equations equal to y, so they can be set equal to one another as:

$$x^2 - 6x + 3 = -2x + 3$$

Moving all terms to the left side results in $x^2 - 4x = 0$. Factoring the expression on the left gives $x(x - 4) = 0$. Setting both factors equal to 0 results in $x = 0$ and $x = 4$. Plugging both x-values into the linear equation results in $y = 3$ and $y = $ -5, respectively. Therefore, the ordered pair solutions are (0, 3) and (4, -5). Both of these ordered pairs satisfy both equations in the original system.

Understanding a Nonlinear Relationship Between Two Variables

Recall that a linear relationship exists between two variables if they are proportional to each other. Basically, if one quantity increases, the other quantity increases or decreases at a constant rate. The graph of a linear relationship is a straight line. If the line goes through the *origin*, the point (0, 0), then there is direct variation between the two quantities and the equation for direct variation is $y = kx$, where k is known as the constant of variation.

Recall also that a nonlinear relationship exists between two variables if an increase in one quantity does not correspond with a constant change in the other quantity. The graphs of nonlinear relationships are not straight lines. Often, the graphs of nonlinear relationships involve curves, where the change in the variable is predictable, but not constant.

A common nonlinear relationship between two variables involves inverse variation where one quantity varies inversely with respect to another. The equation for inverse variation is $y = \frac{k}{x}$, where k is still known as the constant of variation. Here is the graph of the curve $y = \frac{3}{x}$:

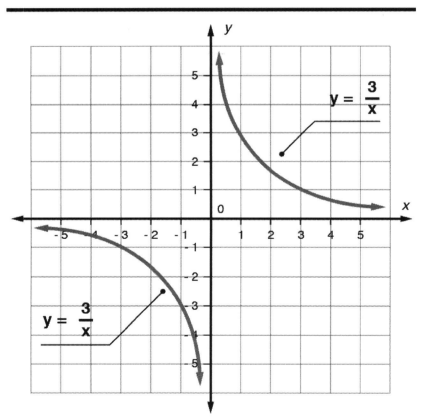

The Graph of $y = \dfrac{3}{x}$

Other common nonlinear functions involve polynomial functions. The squaring function $f(x) = x^2$ can be seen here:

$f(x) = x^2$

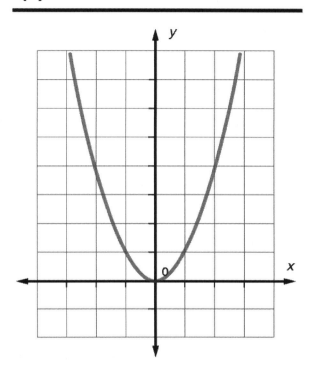

Notice that as the independent variable x increases when $x > 0$, the dependent variable y also increases. However, y does not increase at a constant rate.

Coordinate Geometry

Plane Geometry

Coordinate geometry is the intersection of algebra and geometry. Within this system, the points in a geometric shape are defined using ordered pairs. In the two-dimensional coordinate system, an x- and y-axis form the *xy-plane*. The x-axis is a horizontal scale, and the y-axis is a vertical scale. The ordered pair where the axes cross is known as the *origin*. To the right of the origin, the x values are positive, and to the left of the origin, the x values are negative. The y values above the origin are positive, and y values below the origin are negative. The axes split the plane into four quadrants, and the first quadrant is where both x and y values are positive. To plot an ordered pair means to locate the point corresponding to the x and y coordinates. For example, plotting (4,3) means moving to the right 4 units from 0 in the x direction and then moving up 3 units in the y direction.

Here is a picture of the *xy*-plane, also known as the *rectangular* or *Cartesian coordinate system*.

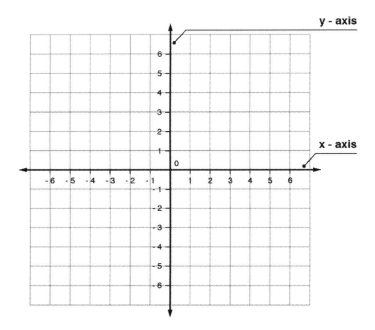

The coordinate system allows us to visualize relationships between equations and geometric figures. For instance, an equation in two variables, *x* and *y*, is represented as a straight line on the *xy* coordinate plane. A solution of an equation in two variables is an ordered pair that satisfies the equation. A graph of an equation can be found by plotting several ordered pairs that are solutions of the equation and then connecting those points with a straight line or smooth curve. Here is the graph of $4x + y = 8$:

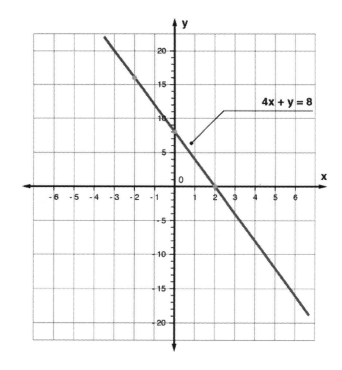

Three ordered pairs that are solutions to the equation were found and plotted. Those points are (–2,16), (0,8), and (2,0). The points were connected using a straight line. Note that the point (0,8) is where the line crosses the y-axis. This point is known as the *y-intercept*. The y-intercept can always be found by plugging $x = 0$ into the equation. Also, the point (2,0) is where the line crosses the x-axis. This point is known as the *x-intercept*, and it can always be found for any equation of a line by plugging $y = 0$ into the equation. The equation above is written in standard form, $Ax + By = C$. Often an equation is written in slope-intercept form, $y = mx + b$, where m represents the slope of the line, and b represents the y-intercept. The above equation can be solved for y to obtain $y = -4x + 8$, which shows a slope of –4 and a y-intercept of 8, meaning the point (0,8).

The *slope* of a line is the measure of steepness of a line, and it compares the vertical change of the line, the *rise*, to the horizontal change of the line, the *run*. The formula for slope of a line through two distinct points (x_1, y_1) and (x_2, y_2) is:

$$m = \frac{y_2 - y_1}{x_2 - x_1}$$

If the line increases from left to right, the slope is positive, and if the line decreases from left to right, as shown above, the slope is negative. If a line is horizontal, like the line representing the equation $y = 5$, the slope is 0. If a line is vertical, like the line representing the equation $x = 2$, the line has undefined slope.

In order to graph a function, it can be done the same way as equations. The $f(x)$ represents the dependent variable y in the equation, so replace $f(x)$ with y and plot some points. For example, the same graph above would be found for the function $f(x) = -4x + 8$. Graphs other than straight lines also exist. For example, here are the graphs of $f(x) = x^2$ and $f(x) = x^3$, the squaring and cubic functions.

$f(x) = x^2$

$f(x) = x^4$

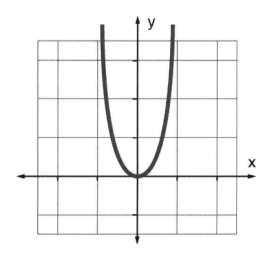

If the equals sign is changed to an inequality symbol such as $<$. $>$, $\leq$, or $\geq$ in an equation, the result is an inequality. If it is changed to a linear equation in two variables, the result is a linear inequality in two variables. A solution of an inequality in two variables is an ordered pair that satisfies the inequality. For example, (1,3) is a solution of the linear inequality $y \geq x + 1$ because when plugged in, it results in a true statement. The graph of an inequality in two variables consists of all ordered pairs that make the solution true. A half-plane consists of the set of all points on one side of a line in the xy-plane, and the solution to a linear inequality is a half-plane. If the inequality consists of > or <, the line is dashed, and no solutions actually exist on the line shown. If the inequality consists of $\geq$ or $\leq$, the line is solid, and solutions do exist on the line shown. In order to graph a linear inequality, graph the corresponding equation found by replacing the inequality symbol with an equals sign. Then pick a test point on either side of the line. If that point results in a true statement when plugged into the original inequality, shade in the side containing the test point. If it results in a false statement, shade in the opposite side. Here is the graph of the inequality $y < x + 1$.

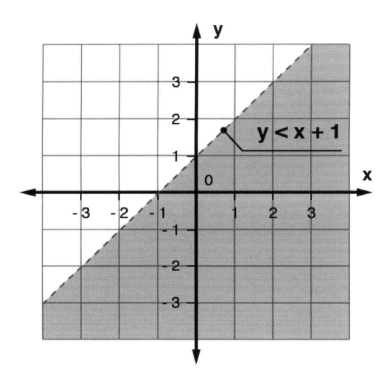

The Coordinate Plane

The coordinate plane is a way of identifying the position of a point in relation to two axes. The *coordinate plane* is made up of two intersecting lines, the x- and y-axis. These lines intersect at a right angle, and their intersection point is called the origin. The points on the coordinate plane are labeled based on their position in relation to the origin. If a point is found 4 units to the right and 2 units up from the origin, the location is described as (4, 2). These numbers are the x- and y-coordinates, always written in the order (x, y). This point is also described as lying in the first quadrant. Every point in the first quadrant has a location that is positive in the x and y directions.

The following figure shows the coordinate plane with examples of points that lie in each quadrant.

The Coordinate Plane

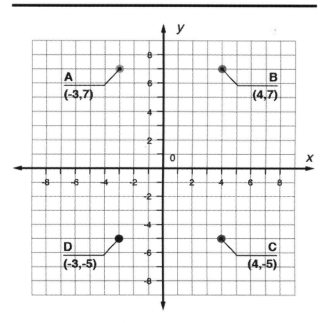

Point B lies in the first quadrant, described positive *x*- and *y*-values, above the *x*-axis and to the right of the *y*-axis. Point A lies in the second quadrant, where the *x*-value is negative and *y*-value is positive. This quadrant is above the *x*-axis and to the left of the *y*-axis. Point D lies in the third quadrant, where both the *x*- and *y*-values are negative. Below the *x*-axis, and to the left of the *y*-axis, is how this quadrant is described. Point C is in the fourth quadrant, where the *x*-value is positive and the *y*-value is negative.

Straight Lines

Geometric figures can be identified by matching the definition with the object. For example, a *line segment* is made up of two endpoints and the line drawn between them. A *ray* is made up of one endpoint and one extending side that goes on forever. A line has no endpoints and two sides that extend on forever. These three geometric figures are shown below. What happens at A and B determines the name of each figure.

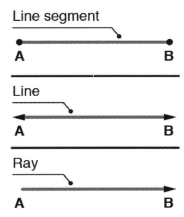

Parallel and perpendicular lines are made up of two lines, like the second figure above. They are distinguished from each other by how the two lines interact. *Parallel* lines run alongside one another, but they never intersect. *Perpendicular* lines intersect at a 90-degree, or a right, angle. An example of these two sets of lines is show below. Also shown in the figure are non-examples of these two types of lines. Because the first set of lines, in the top left corner, will eventually intersect if they continue, they are not parallel. In the second set, the lines run in the same direction and will never intersect, making them parallel. The third set, in the bottom left corner, intersect at an angle that is not right, or not 90 degrees. The fourth set is perpendicular because it intersects at exactly a right angle.

Lines

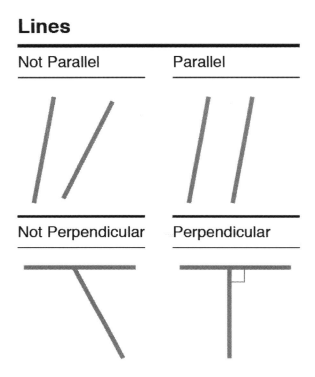

| Not Parallel | Parallel |

| Not Perpendicular | Perpendicular |

Conics

The intersection of a plane and a double right circular cone is called a *conic section*. There are four basic types of conic sections, a circle, a parabola, a hyperbola, and an ellipse. The equation of a circle is given by $(x - h)^2 + (y - k)^2 = r^2$, where the center of the circle is given by (h, k) and the radius of the circle is 5. A parabola that opens up or down has a horizontal axis. The equation of a parabola with a horizontal axis is given by $(y - k)^2 = 4p(x - h)$, p ≠ 0, where the vertex is given by (h, k). A parabola that opens to the left or right has a vertical axis. The equation of the parabola with a vertical axis is given by $(x - h)^2 = 4p(y - k)$, p≠0, where the vertex is given by (h, k). The equation of an ellipse with a horizontal major axis is given by $\frac{(x-h)^2}{a^2} + \frac{(y-k)^2}{b^2} = 1$, with center ($h$, k). The distance between center and either focus is c with $c^2 = a^2 - b^2$, a > b > 0. The major axis has length 2a and the minor axis has length 2b. For an ellipse with a vertical major axis, the a and b switch places so the equation is given by $\frac{(x-h)^2}{b^2} + \frac{(y-k)^2}{a^2} = 1$, a >b > 0, with center (h, k). The major axis still has length 2a and the minor axis still has length 2b, and the distance between center and either focus is $c^2 = a^2 - b^2$, a > b > 0. A hyperbola has an equation similar to the ellipse except that there is a minus in place of the plus sign. A hyperbola with a vertical transverse axis has equation: $\frac{(x-h)^2}{a^2} - \frac{(y-k)^2}{b^2} = 1$, and a hyperbola with a horizontal transverse axis has equation:

$$\frac{(y-k)^2}{a^2} - \frac{(x-h)^2}{b^2} = 1$$

For each of these, the center is given by (h, k) and distance between the vertices $2a$.

Sets of Points in the Plane

Shapes can be plotted on the coordinate plane to identify location of each vertex and the length of each side. The original shape is seen in the figure below in the first quadrant. The length is 6 and the width is 4. The reflection of this rectangle is in the fourth quadrant. A reflection across the y-axis can be found by determining each point's distance to the y-axis and moving it that same distance on the opposite side. For example, the point C is located at (2, 1). The reflection of this point moves to (–2, 1) when reflected across the y-axis. The original point A is located at (2, 5), and the reflection across the y-axis is located at (–2, 5). It is evident that the reflection across the y-axis changes the sign of the x-coordinate. A reflection across the x-axis changes the sign on the y-coordinate, as seen in the reflected figure below. Other translations can be found using the coordinate plane, such as rotations around the origin and reflections across the y-axis.

Circles in the Coordinate Plane
Recall that a circle is the set of all points the same distance, known as radius r, from a single point C, known as the center of the circle. The center has coordinates (h, k) and any point on the circle is an ordered pair with coordinates (x, y). A right triangle with hypotenuse r can be formed with these two points as seen here:

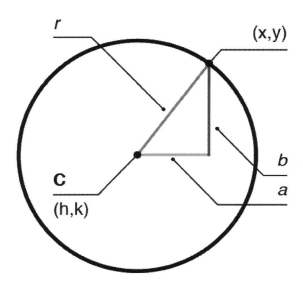

The other side lengths are a and b. The Pythagorean Theorem states that $a^2 + b^2 = r^2$. However, a can be replaced by $|x - h|$ and b can be replaced by $|y - k|$ because the distance between any two coordinates in the coordinate plane is the absolute value of their difference. That substitution gives $(x - h)^2 + (y - k)^2 = r^2$, which is the formula used to find the equation of any circle with center (h, k) and radius r.

Therefore, if any problem gives the coordinates of the center of a circle and its radius length, this is the equation in two variables that allows any other point on the circle to be found.

Oftentimes, the center or the radius of a circle are not easily seen in the given equation of the circle. If the equation is in standard form of a polynomial equation like $ax^2 + ay^2 + cx + dy + e = 0$, the algebraic technique of completing the square must be used to find the coordinates of the center and the radius. Completing the square must be done within both variables x and y. First, the constant term needs to be subtracted off of both sides of the equation, and then the x and y terms need to be grouped together. Then, the entire equation needs to be divided by a. Then, divide the coefficient of the x-term by 2, square it, and add that value to both sides of the equation.. This value should be grouped with the x terms. Next, divide the coefficient of the y-term by 2, square it, and add it to both sides of the equation, grouping it with the y terms. The trinomial in both x and y are now perfect square trinomials and can be factored into squares of a binomial. This process results in $(x - h)^2 + (y - k)^2 = r^2$, showing the radius and coordinates of the center.

Applications and Other Algebra Topics

Complex Numbers

A *complex number* is of the form $a + bi$, where a and b are real numbers and i is the imaginary number, $\sqrt{-1}$. The real part of the number is a, and the imaginary part is bi. To add two complex numbers, add the real parts together and the imaginary parts together, similar to combining like terms in polynomials. For example, $(3 + 4i) + (4 - 3i) = 7 + i$. Subtraction is done in a similar manner, by adding the opposite of the second number. For example, $(3 + 4i) - (4 - 3i) = (3 + 4i) + (-4 + 3i) = -1 + 7i$. Multiplication is performed the same way as multiplying polynomials, through foiling and collecting like terms. Remember that $i^2 = -1$. Therefore, $(3 + 4i)(4 - 3i) = 12 - 9i + 16i - 12i^2 = 12 + 7i + 12 = 24 + 7i$. Simplifying complex numbers involves combining like terms: real parts with real parts and imaginary parts with imaginary parts.

The *conjugate* of a complex number $a + bi$ is $a - bi$. Note that when a complex number is multiplied times its conjugate, the result is $(a + bi)(a - bi) = a^2 - b^2i^2 = a^2 + b^2$, and its square root is known as the *magnitude*, or *absolute value*, of the number. To divide a complex number by another complex number, multiply the numerator and the denominator of the expression times the conjugate of the denominator. Here is an example of a complex number division problem:

A Complex Number Division Problem

$$\frac{2 + 3i}{4 - 5i} = \frac{2 + 3i}{4 - 5i} \times \frac{4 + 5i}{4 + 5i} =$$

$$= \frac{8 + 10i + 12i + 15i^2}{16 + 20i - 20i - 25i^2} =$$

$$= \frac{8 + 22i + 15 \times (-1)}{16 - 25 \times (-1)} =$$

$$= \frac{-7 + 22i}{49} =$$

$$= -\frac{7}{49} + \frac{22}{49} i$$

Series and Sequences

A *sequence of numbers* is a list of numbers that follows a specific pattern. Each member of the sequence is known as an *individual term* of the sequence, and a formula can be found to represent each term. For example, the list of numbers $1, 5, 10, 15, \dots$ is a sequence of numbers, and ... shows that the sequence continues indefinitely. Each term represents a multiple of 5. The first term is 1×5, the second term is 2×5, the third term is 3×5, etc. In general, the nth term is $3 \times n$. Other, more complicated, sequences can exist as well. For example, each term of the sequence 1, 4, 9, 16, 25, ... is not found through addition or multiplication. Each term happens to be a perfect square, and the first term is 1 squared, the second term is 2 squared, etc. Therefore, the nth term is n^2. A famous sequence of numbers is the Fibonacci sequence, which consists of 0, 1, 1, 2, 3, 5, 8, 13, 21, ... After the first two terms 0 and 1, all terms are found by adding the two previous terms. Therefore, the next term in the sequence is $13 + 21 = 34$. The formula for the nth term is defined recursively, using the two previous terms.

Patterns in math are those sets of numbers or shapes that follow a rule. Given a set of values, patterns allow the question of "what's next?" to be answered. In the following set there are two types of shapes, a lighter rectangle and a darker circle. The set contains a pattern because every odd-placed shape is a lighter rectangle and every even-placed spot is taken by a darker circle. This is a pattern because there is a rule of lighter rectangle, then darker circle, that is followed to find the set.

A set of numbers can also be described as having a pattern if there is a rule that can be followed to reproduce the set. The following set of numbers has a rule of adding 3 each time. It begins with zero and increases by 3 each time. By following this rule and pattern, the number after 12 is found to be 15. Further extending the pattern, the number are 18, 21, 24, 27. The pattern of increasing by multiples of three can describe this pattern.

A pattern can also be generated from a given rule. Starting with zero, the rule of adding 5 can be used to produce a set of numbers. The following list will result from using the rule: 0, 5, 10, 15, 20. Describing this pattern can include words such as "multiples" of 5 and an "increase" of 5. Any time this pattern needs to be extended, the rule can be applied to find more numbers. Patterns are identified by the rules they follow. This rule should be able to generate new numbers or shapes, while also applying to the given numbers or shapes.

Making Conjectures, Predictions, and Generalizations Based on Patterns
Given a certain pattern, future numbers or shapes can be found. Pascal's triangle is an example of a pattern of numbers. Questions can be asked of the triangle, such as, "what comes next?" and "what values determine the next line?" By examining the different parts of the triangle, conjectures can be made about how the numbers are generated. For the first few rows of numbers, the increase is small. Then the numbers begin to increase more quickly. By looking at each row, a conjecture can be made that the sum of the first row determines the second row's numbers. The second row's numbers can be added to find the third row. To test this conjecture, two numbers can be added, and the number found directly between and below them should be that sum. For the third row, the middle number is 2, which is the sum of the two 1s above it. For the fifth row, the 1 and 3 can be added to find a sum of 4, the same number below the 1 and 3. This pattern continues throughout the triangle. Once the pattern is confirmed to apply throughout the triangle, predictions can be made for future rows. The sums of the bottom row numbers can be found and then added to the bottom of the triangle. In more general terms, the diagonal rows have patterns as well. The outside numbers are always 1. The second diagonal rows are in counting order. The third diagonal row increases each time by one more than the previous. It is helpful to generalize patterns because it makes the pattern more useful in terms of applying it. Pascal's triangle can be used to predict the tossing of a coin, predicting the chances of heads or tails for different numbers of tosses. It

can also be used to show the Fibonacci Sequence, which is found by adding the diagonal numbers together.

Pascal's Triangle

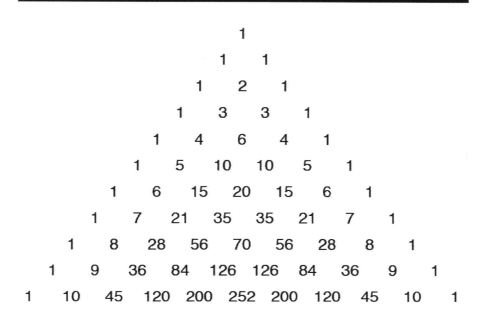

```
                          1
                      1       1
                  1       2       1
              1       3       3       1
          1       4       6       4       1
      1       5      10      10       5       1
  1       6      15      20      15       6       1
1       7      21      35      35      21       7       1
  1   8      28      56      70      56      28       8      1
1   9      36      84     126     126     84      36      9      1
1  10     45     120    200    252    200    120     45     10     1
```

Identifying Relationships Between the Corresponding Terms of Two Numerical Patterns
Sets of numerical patterns can be found by starting with a number and following a given rule. If two sets are generated, the corresponding terms in each set can be found to relate to one another by one or more operations. For example, the following table shows two sets of numbers that each follow their own pattern. The first column shows a pattern of numbers increasing by 1. The second column shows the numbers increasing by 4. Because the numbers are lined up, corresponding numbers are side by side for the two sets. A question to ask is, "How can the number in the first column be turned into the number in the second column?"

1	4
2	8
3	12
4	16
5	20

This answer will lead to the relationship between the two sets. By recognizing the multiples of 4 in the right column and the counting numbers in order in the left column, the relationship of multiplying by four is determined. The first set is multiplied by 4 to get the second set of numbers. To confirm this relationship, each set of corresponding numbers can be checked. For any two sets of numerical patterns, the corresponding numbers can be lined up to find how each one relates to the other. In some cases, the relationship is simply addition or subtraction, multiplication or division. In other relationships, these operations are used in conjunction with each together. As seen in the following table, the relationship uses multiplication and addition. The following expression shows this relationship: $3x + 2$. The x represents the numbers in the first column.

1	5
2	8
3	11
4	14

Determinants

A *matrix* is an arrangement of numbers in rows and columns. Matrices are used to work with vectors and transform them. One example is a system of linear equations. Matrices can represent a system and be used to transform and solve the system. An important connection between scalars, vectors, and matrices is this: scalars are only numbers, vectors are numbers with magnitude and direction, and matrices are an array of numbers in rows and columns. The rows run from left to right and the columns run from top to bottom. When describing the dimensions of a matrix, the number of rows is stated first and the number of columns is stated second. The following matrix has two rows and three columns, referred to as a 2×3 matrix: $\begin{matrix} 3 & 5 & 7 \\ 4 & 2 & 8 \end{matrix}$. A number in a matrix can be found by describing its location. For example, the number in row two, column three is 8. In row one, column two, the number 5 is found.

Operations can be performed on matrices, just as they can on vectors. Scalar multiplication can be performed on matrices and it will change the magnitude, just as with a vector. A scalar multiplication problem using a 2×2 matrix looks like the following: $3 \times \begin{bmatrix} 4 & 5 \\ 8 & 3 \end{bmatrix}$. The scalar of 3 is multiplied by each number to form the resulting matrix: $\begin{bmatrix} 12 & 15 \\ 24 & 9 \end{bmatrix}$. Matrices can also be added and subtracted. For these operations to be performed, the matrices must be the same dimensions. Other operations that can be performed to manipulate matrices are multiplication, division, and transposition. *Transposing* a matrix means to switch the rows and columns. If the original matrix has two rows and three columns, then the transposed matrix has three rows and two columns.

Permutations and Combinations

A *probability experiment* is an action that causes specific results, such as counts or measurements. The result of such an experiment is known as an *outcome*, and the set of all potential outcomes is known as the *sample space*. An *event* consists of one or more of those outcomes. For example, consider the probability experiment of tossing a coin and rolling a six-sided die. The coin has two possible outcomes—a heads or a tails—and the die has six possible outcomes—rolling each number 1–6. Therefore, the sample space has twelve possible outcomes: a heads or a tails paired with each roll of the die.

A *simple event* is an event that consists of a single outcome. For instance, selecting a queen of hearts from a standard fifty-two-card deck is a simple event; however, selecting a queen is not a simple event because there are four possibilities.

Classical, or *theoretical*, *probability* is when each outcome in a sample space has the same chance to occur. The probability for an event is equal to the number of outcomes in that event divided by the total number of outcomes in the sample space. For example, consider rolling a six-sided die. The probability of rolling a 2 is $\frac{1}{6}$, and the probability of rolling an even number is $\frac{3}{6}$, or $\frac{1}{2}$, because there are three even numbers on the die. This type of probability is based on what should happen in theory but not what actually happens in real life.

Empirical probability is based on actual experiments or observations. For example, if a die is rolled eight times, and a 1 is rolled two times, the empirical probability of rolling a 1 is $\frac{2}{8} = \frac{1}{4}$, which is higher than the theoretical probability. The Law of Large Numbers states that as an experiment is completed repeatedly, the empirical probability of an event should get closer to the theoretical probability of an event.

Probabilities range from 0 to 1. The closer something is to 0, the less likely it will occur. The closer it is to 1, the more likely it is to occur.

The *addition rule* is necessary to find the probability of event A or event B occurring or both occurring at the same time. If events A and B are *mutually exclusive* or *disjoint*, which means they cannot occur at the same time, $P(A \text{ or } B) = P(A) + P(B)$. If events A and B are not mutually exclusive, $P(A \text{ or } B) = P(A) + P(B) - P(A \text{ and } B)$ where $P(A \text{ and } B)$ represents the probability of event A and B both occurring at the same time. An example of two events that are mutually exclusive are rolling a 6 on a die and rolling an odd number on a die. The probability of rolling a 6 or rolling an odd number is $\frac{1}{6} + \frac{3}{6} = \frac{4}{6} = \frac{2}{3}$. Rolling a 6 and rolling an even number are not mutually exclusive because there is some overlap. The probability of rolling a 6 or rolling an even number is $\frac{1}{6} + \frac{3}{6} - \frac{1}{6} = \frac{3}{6} = \frac{1}{2}$.

Conditional Probability

The *multiplication rule* is necessary when finding the probability that an event A occurs in a first trial and event B occurs in a second trial, which is written as $P(A \text{ and } B)$. This rule differs if the events are independent or dependent. Two events A and B are *independent* if the occurrence of one event does not affect the probability that the other will occur. If A and B are not independent, they are *dependent*, and the outcome of the first event somehow affects the outcome of the second. If events A and B are independent, $P(A \text{ and } B) = P(A)P(B)$, and if events A and B are dependent, $P(A \text{ and } B) = P(A)P(B|A)$, where $P(B|A)$ represents the probability event B occurs given that event A has already occurred.

$P(B|A)$ represents *conditional probability*, or the probability of event B occurring given that event A has already occurred. $P(B|A)$ can be found by dividing the probability of events A and B both occurring by the probability of event A occurring using the formula $P(B|A) = \frac{P(A \text{ and } B)}{P(A)}$ and represents the total number of outcomes remaining for B to occur after A occurs. This formula is derived from the multiplication rule with dependent events by dividing both sides by $P(A)$. Note that $P(B|A)$ and $P(A|B)$ are not the same. The first quantity shows that event B has occurred after event A, and the second quantity shows that event A has occurred after event B. To incorrectly interchange these ideas is known as *confusion of the inverse*.

Consider the case of drawing two cards from a deck of fifty-two cards. The probability of pulling two queens would vary based on whether the initial card was placed back in the deck for the second pull. If the card is placed back in, the probability of pulling two queens is $\frac{4}{52} \times \frac{4}{52} = 0.00592$. If the card is not placed back in, the probability of pulling two queens is $\frac{4}{52} \times \frac{3}{51} = 0.00452$. When the card is not placed back in, both the numerator and denominator of the second probability decrease by 1. This is due to the fact that, theoretically, there is one less queen in the deck, and there is one less total card in the deck as well.

Conditional probability is used frequently when probabilities are calculated from tables. Two-way frequency tables display data with two variables and highlight the relationships between those two variables. They are often used to summarize survey results and are also known as *contingency tables*. Each cell shows a count pertaining to that individual variable pairing, known as a *joint frequency*, and the totals of each row and column also are in the tables. Consider the following two-way frequency table:

	70 or older	**69 or younger**	**Totals**
Women	20	40	60
Men	5	35	40
Total	25	75	100

This table shows the breakdown of ages and sexes of 100 people in a particular village. Consider a randomly selected villager. The probability of selecting a male 69 years old or younger is $\frac{35}{100}$ because there are 35 males under the age of 70 and 100 total villagers.

Probability Distributions

A *discrete random variable* is a set of values that is either finite or countably infinite. If there are infinitely many values, being *countable* means that each individual value can be paired with a natural number. For example, the number of coin tosses before getting heads could potentially be infinite, but the total number of tosses is countable. Each toss refers to a number, like the first toss, second toss, etc. A *continuous random variable* has infinitely many values that are not countable. The individual items cannot be enumerated; an example of such a set is any type of measurement. There are infinitely many heights of human beings due to decimals that exist within each inch, centimeter, millimeter, etc. Each type of variable has its own *probability distribution*, which calculates the probability for each potential value of the random variable. Probability distributions exist in tables, formulas, or graphs. The expected value of a random variable represents what the mean value should be in either a large sample size or after many trials. According to the Law of Large Numbers, after many trials, the actual mean and that of the probability distribution should be very close to the expected value. The *expected value* is a weighted average that is calculated as $E(X) = \sum x_i p_i$, where x_i represents the value of each outcome, and p_i represents the probability of each outcome. The expected value if all of the probabilities are equal is $E(X) = \frac{x_1 + x_2 + \cdots + x_n}{n}$. Expected value is often called the *mean of the random variable* and is known as a *measure of central tendency* like mean and mode.

A *binomial probability distribution* is a probability distribution that adheres to some important criteria. The distribution must consist of a fixed number of trials where all trials are independent, each trial has an outcome classified as either success or failure, and the probability of a success is the same in each trial. Within any binomial experiment, *x* is the number of resulting successes, *n* is the number of trials, *P* is the probability of success within each trial, and $Q = 1 - P$ is the probability of failure within each trial. The probability of obtaining *x* successes within *n* trials is $\binom{n}{x} P^x (1 - P)^{n-x}$, where $\binom{n}{x} = \frac{n!}{x!(n-x)!}$ is called the *binomial coefficient*. A binomial probability distribution could be used to find the probability of obtaining exactly two heads on five tosses of a coin. In the formula, $x = 2$, $n = 5$, $P = 0.5$, and $Q = 0.5$.

A *uniform probability distribution* exists when there is constant probability. Each random variable has equal probability, and its graph is a rectangle because the height, representing the probability, is constant.

Finally, a *normal probability distribution* has a graph that is symmetric and bell-shaped; an example using body weight is shown here:

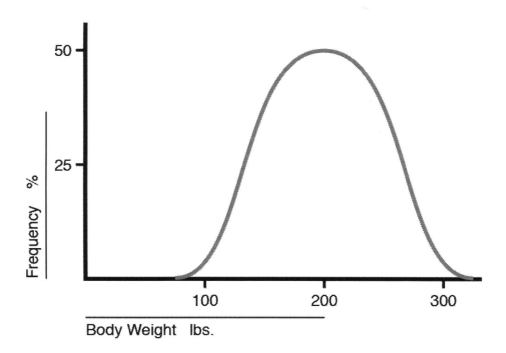

Population percentages can be estimated using normal distributions. For example, the probability that a data point will be less than the mean is 50 percent. The Empirical Rule states that 68 percent of the data falls within 1 standard deviation of the mean, 95 percent falls within 2 standard deviations of the mean, and 99.7 percent falls within 3 standard deviations of the mean. A *standard normal distribution* is a normal distribution with a mean equal to 0 and standard deviation equal to 1. The area under the entire curve of a standard normal distribution is equal to 1.

Counting Methods

Probability problems require that the total number of events in the sample space must be known. Different methods can be used to count the number of possible outcomes, depending on whether different arrangements of the same items are counted only once or separately. *Permutations* are arrangements in which different sequences are counted separately. Therefore, order matters in permutations. *Combinations* are arrangements in which different sequences are not counted separately. Therefore, order does not matter in combinations. For example, if 123 is considered different from 321, permutations would be discussed. However, if 123 is considered the same as 321, combinations would be considered.

If the sample space contains n different permutations of n different items and all of them must be selected, there are $n!$ different possibilities. For example, five different books can be rearranged $5! = 120$ times. The probability of one person randomly ordering those five books in the same way as another person is $\frac{1}{120}$. A different calculation is necessary if a number less than n is to be selected or if order does not matter. In general, the notation $P(n, r)$ represents the number of ways to arrange r objects from a set of n if order does matter, and:

$$P(n, r) = \frac{n!}{(n - r)!}$$

Therefore, in order to calculate the number of ways five books can be arranged in three slots if order matters, plug $n = 5$ and $r = 3$ in the formula to obtain:

$$P(5,3) = \frac{5!}{(5 - 3)!} = \frac{5!}{2!} = 60$$

Secondly, $C(n, r)$ represents the total number of r combinations selected out of n items when order does not matter, and:

$$C(n, r) = \frac{n!}{(n - r)! \; r!}$$

Therefore, the number of ways five books can be arranged in three slots if order does not matter is:

$$C(5,3) = \frac{5!}{(5 - 3)! \; 3!} = 10$$

The following relationship exists between permutations and combinations:

$$C(n, r) = \frac{P(n, r)}{r!}$$

Sets of numbers and other similarly organized data can also be represented graphically. Venn diagrams are a common way to do so. A Venn diagram represents each set of data as a circle. The circles overlap, showing that each set of data is overlapping. A Venn diagram is also known as a *logic diagram* because it visualizes all possible logical combinations between two sets. Common elements of two sets are represented by the area of overlap. The following is an example of a Venn diagram of two sets A and B:

Parts of the Venn Diagram

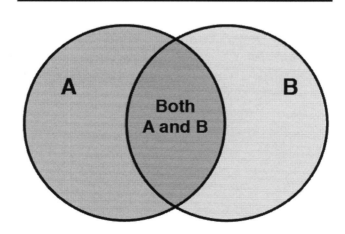

Another name for the area of overlap is the *intersection*. The intersection of A and B, $A \cap B$, contains all elements that are in both sets A and B. The union of A and B, $A \cup B$, contains all elements that are in either set A or set B. Finally, the complement of $A \cup B$ is equal to all elements that are not in either set A or set B. These elements are placed outside of the circles.

The following is an example of a Venn diagram in which 24 students were surveyed asking if they had brothers or sisters or both. Ten students only had brothers, 7 students only had sisters, and 5 had both brothers and sisters. This number 5 is the intersection and is placed where the circles overlap. Two students did not have a cat or a dog. Two is therefore the complement and is placed outside of the circles.

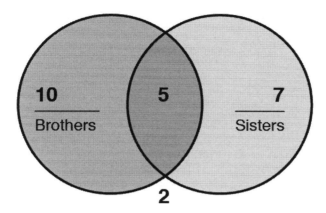

Venn diagrams can have more than two sets of data. The more circles, the more logical combinations are represented by the overlapping. The following is a Venn diagram that represents students who like the colors green, pink, or blue. There were 30 students surveyed. The innermost region represents those students that like green, pink, and blue. Therefore, 2 students like all three. In this example, all students like at least one of the colors, so no one exists in the complement.

30 students

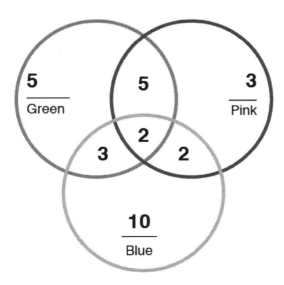

Venn diagrams are typically not drawn to scale, but if they are and their area is proportional to the amount of data it represents, it is known as an *area-proportional* Venn diagram.

Fractions

Recall that a rational number can be written as a fraction and can be converted to a decimal through division. If a rational number is negative, the rules for adding, subtracting, multiplying, and dividing integers must be used. If a rational number is in fraction form, performing addition, subtraction, multiplication, and division is more complicated than when working with integers. First, consider addition. To add two fractions having the same denominator, add the numerators and then reduce the fraction. When an answer is a fraction, it should always be in lowest terms. *Lowest terms* means that every common factor, other than 1, between the numerator and denominator is divided out. For example, $\frac{2}{8} + \frac{4}{8} = \frac{6}{8} = \frac{6 \div 2}{8 \div 2} = \frac{3}{4}$. Both the numerator and denominator of $\frac{6}{8}$ have a common factor of 2, so 2 is divided out of each number to put the fraction in lowest terms. If denominators are different in an addition problem, the fractions must be converted to have common denominators. The *least common denominator (LCD)* of all the given denominators must be found, and this value is equal to the *least common multiple (LCM)* of the denominators. This non-zero value is the smallest number that is a multiple of both denominators. Then, rewrite each original fraction as an equivalent fraction using the new denominator. Once in this form, apply the process of adding with like denominators. For example, consider $\frac{1}{3} + \frac{4}{9}$. The LCD is 9 because it is the smallest multiple of both 3 and 9. The fraction $\frac{1}{3}$ must be rewritten with 9 as its denominator. Therefore, multiply both the numerator and denominator times 3. Multiplying times $\frac{3}{3}$ is the same as multiplying times 1, which does not change the value of the fraction. Therefore, an equivalent fraction is $\frac{3}{9}$, and $\frac{1}{3} + \frac{4}{9} = \frac{3}{9} + \frac{4}{9} = \frac{7}{9}$, which is in lowest terms. Subtraction is performed in a similar manner; once the denominators are equal, the numerators are then subtracted. The following is an example of addition of a positive and a negative fraction:

$$-\frac{5}{12} + \frac{5}{9} = -\frac{5 \times 3}{12 \times 3} + \frac{5 \times 4}{9 \times 4} = -\frac{15}{36} + \frac{20}{36} = \frac{5}{36}$$

Common denominators are not used in multiplication and division. To multiply two fractions, multiply the numerators together and the denominators together. Then, write the result in lowest terms. For example, $\frac{2}{3} \times \frac{9}{4} = \frac{18}{12} = \frac{3}{2}$. Alternatively, the fractions could be factored first to cancel out any common factors before performing the multiplication. For example, $\frac{2}{3} \times \frac{9}{4} = \frac{2}{3} \times \frac{3 \times 3}{2 \times 2} = \frac{3}{2}$. This second approach is helpful when working with larger numbers, as common factors might not be obvious. Multiplication and division of fractions are related because the division of two fractions is changed into a multiplication problem. Division of a fraction is equivalent to multiplication of the *reciprocal* of the second fraction, so that second fraction must be inverted, or "flipped," to be in reciprocal form. For example, $\frac{11}{15} \div \frac{3}{5} = \frac{11}{15} \times \frac{5}{3} = \frac{55}{45} = \frac{11}{9}$. The fraction $\frac{5}{3}$ is the reciprocal of $\frac{3}{5}$. It is possible to multiply and divide numbers containing a mix of integers and fractions. In this case, convert the integer to a fraction by placing it over a denominator of 1. For example, a division problem involving an integer and a fraction is $3 \div \frac{1}{2} = \frac{3}{1} \times \frac{2}{1} = \frac{6}{1} = 6$. Finally, when performing operations with rational numbers that are negative, the same rules apply as when performing operations with integers. For example, a negative fraction times a negative fraction results in a positive value, and a negative fraction subtracted from a negative fraction results in a negative value.

Word Problems

One-step problems take only one mathematical step to solve. For example, solving the equation $5x = 45$ is a one-step problem because the one step of dividing both sides of the equation by 5 is the only step necessary to obtain the solution $x = 9$. The multiplication principle of equality is the one step used to isolate the variable. The equation is of the form $ax = b$, where a and b are rational numbers. Similarly, the addition principle of equality could be the one step needed to solve a problem. In this case, the equation would be of the form $x + a = b$ or $x - a = b$, for real numbers a and b.

A multi-step problem involves more than one step to find the solution, or it could consist of solving more than one equation. An equation that involves both the addition principle and the multiplication principle is a two-step problem, and an example of such an equation is $2x - 4 = 5$. Solving involves adding 4 to both sides and then dividing both sides by 2. An example of a two-step problem involving two separate equations is $y = 3x, 2x + y = 4$. The two equations form a system of two equations that must be solved together in two variables. The system can be solved by the substitution method. Since y is already solved for in terms of x, plug $3x$ in for y into the equation $2x + y = 4$, resulting in $2x + 3x = 4$. Therefore, $5x = 4$ and $x = \frac{4}{5}$. Because there are two variables, the solution consists of both a value for x and for y. Substitute $x = \frac{4}{5}$ into either original equation to find y. The easiest choice is $y = 3x$. Therefore, $y = 3 \times \frac{4}{5} = \frac{12}{5}$. The solution can be written as the ordered pair $\left(\frac{4}{5}, \frac{12}{5}\right)$.

Real-world problems can be translated into both one-step and multi-step problems. In either case, the word problem must be translated from the verbal form into mathematical expressions and equations that can be solved using algebra. An example of a one-step real-world problem is the following: A cat weighs half as much as a dog living in the same house. If the dog weighs 14.5 pounds, how much does the cat weigh? To solve this problem, an equation can be used. In any word problem, the first step must be defining variables that represent the unknown quantities. For this problem, let x be equal to the unknown weight of the cat. Because two times the weight of the cat equals 14.5 pounds, the equation to be solved is: $2x = 14.5$. Use the multiplication principle to divide both sides by 2. Therefore, $x = 7.25$. The cat weighs 7.25 pounds.

Most of the time, real-world problems are more difficult than this one and consist of multi-step problems. The following is an example of a multi-step problem: The sum of two consecutive page numbers is equal to 437. What are those page numbers? First, define the unknown quantities. If x is equal to the first page number, then $x + 1$ is equal to the next page number because they are consecutive integers. Their sum is equal to 437, and this statement translates to the equation $x + x + 1 = 437$. To solve, first collect like terms to obtain $2x + 1 = 437$. Then, subtract 1 from both sides and then divide by 2. The solution to the equation is $x = 218$. Therefore, the two consecutive page numbers that satisfy the problem are 218 and 219. It is always important to make sure that answers to real-world problems make sense. For instance, if the solution to this same problem resulted in decimals, that should be a red flag indicating the need to check the work. Page numbers are whole numbers; therefore, if decimals are found to be answers, the solution process should be double-checked to see where mistakes were made.

Solving Problems
To solve problems, follow these steps: Identify the variables that are known, decide which equation should be used, substitute the numbers, and solve. To solve an equation for the amount of time that has elapsed since an event, use the equation $T = L - E$ where T represents the elapsed time, L represents the later time, and E represents the earlier time. For example, the Minnesota Vikings have not appeared in the Super Bowl since 1976. If the year is now 2017, how long has it been since the Vikings were in the Super Bowl? The later time, L, is 2017, $E = 1976$ and the unknown is T. Substituting these numbers, the equation is T =

2017 − 1976, and so T = 41. It has been 41 years since the Vikings have appeared in the Super Bowl. Questions involving total cost can be solved using the formula, C = I + T where C represents the total cost, I represents the cost of the item purchased, and T represents the tax amount. To find the length of a rectangle given the area = 32 square inches and width = 8 inches, the formula A = L × W can be used. Substitute 32 for A and substitute 8 for w, giving the equation 32 = L×8. This equation is solved by dividing both sides by 8 to find that the length of the rectangle is 4. The formula for volume of a rectangular prism is given by the equation V = L × W × H. If the length of a rectangular juice box is 4 centimeters, the width is 2 centimeters, and the height is 8 centimeters, what is the volume of this box? Substituting in the formula we find V = 4 × 2 × 8, so the volume is 64 cubic centimeters. In a similar fashion as those previously shown, the mass of an object can be calculated given the formula, Mass = Density × Volume.

Functions and Trigonometry

Relations, Functions, Equations, and Inequalities

In math, a *relation* is a relationship between two sets of numbers. By using a rule, it takes a number from the first set and matches it to a number in the second set. A relation consists of a set of inputs, known as the *domain*, and a set of outputs, known as the *range*. A *function* is a relation in which each member of the domain is paired to only one other member of the range. In other words, each input has only one output.

Here is an example of a relation that is not a function:

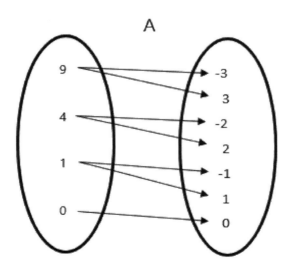

Every member of the first set, the domain, is mapped to two members of the second set, the range. Therefore, this relation is not a function.

In addition to a diagram representing sets, a function can be represented by a table of ordered pairs, a graph of ordered pairs (a scatterplot), or a set of ordered pairs as shown in the following:

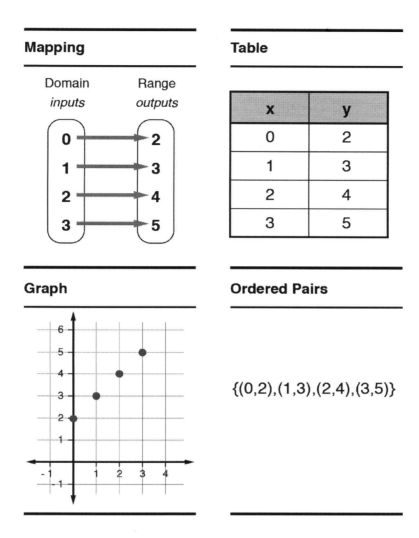

Mapping

Domain — inputs

Range — outputs

0 → 2
1 → 3
2 → 4
3 → 5

Table

x	y
0	2
1	3
2	4
3	5

Graph

Ordered Pairs

$\{(0,2),(1,3),(2,4),(3,5)\}$

Note that this relation is a function because every member of the domain is mapped to exactly one member of the range.

An *equation* occurs when two algebraic expressions are set equal to one another. Functions can be represented in equation form. Given an equation in two variables, x and y, it can be expressed in function form if solved for y. For example, the linear equation $2x + y = 5$ can be solved for y to obtain $y = -2x + 5$, otherwise known as *slope-intercept* form. To place the equation in function form, replace y with $f(x)$, which is read "f of x." Therefore, $f(x) = -2x + 5$. This notation clarifies the input–output relationship of the function. The function f is a function of x, so an x value can be plugged into the function to obtain an output. For example, $f(2) = -2 \times 2 + 5 = 1$. Therefore, an input of 2 corresponds to an output of 1.

A function can be graphed by plotting ordered pairs in the *xy*-plane in the same way that the equation form is graphed. The graph of a function always passes the *Vertical Line Test*. Basically, for any graph, if a vertical line can be drawn through any part of the graph and it hits the graph in more than one place, the graph is not a function. For example, the graph of a circle is not a function. The Vertical Line Test shows that with these relationships, the same x value has more than one y value, which goes against the definition of a function.

Inequalities look like equations, but instead of an equals sign, $<, >, \leq, \geq$, or $\neq$ are used. Here are some examples of inequalities: $2x + 7 < y, 3x^2 \geq 5$, and $x \neq 4$. Inequalities show relationships between algebraic expressions when the quantities are different. Inequalities can also be expressed in function form if they are solved for y. For instance, the first inequality listed above can be written as $2x + y < f(x)$.

Even and Odd Functions

A function is considered *even* when $f(x) = f(-x)$ for all values of x. This relationship means that the graph of an even function is perfectly symmetrical about the y-axis. In other words, the graph is reflected over the y-axis. The term "even" describes these functions because functions like x^2, x^4, x^6, and so on display this characteristic. That said, there are some functions that are even that don't involve x raised to an even exponent. For example, the graph of $f(x) = cos(x)$ is also symmetrical over the y-axis. There are also function that *do* have an even exponent that are *not* even functions; although $f(x) = x^2 + 3$ is an even function, $f(x) = (x + 3)^2$ is not because $f(x) \neq f(-x)$ for all values of x.

A function is considered *odd* when $-f(x) = f(-x)$ for all values of x. This relationship means that the graph of an odd function is perfectly symmetrical about the origin. The term "odd" describes these functions because functions like x, x^3, x^5, x^7, and so on display this characteristic. As with even functions, exceptions to these exponential values exist. For example, the graph of $f(x) = sin(x)$ also has origin symmetry. There are also function that *do* have an odd exponent that are *not* odd functions; while $f(x) = x^3 - 3x$ is an odd function, $f(x) = x^3 - 1$ is not because $-f(x) \neq f(-x)$ for all values of x.

The majority of functions do not display these unique relationships and are thus neither even nor odd. Essentially, to algebraically determine if a function is even, odd, or neither, various values need to be plugged in for $f(x)$ and $f(-x)$. If all values of x yield the same output for $f(x)$ and $f(-x)$, the function is even. If all values of x yield the same output for $-f(x)$ and $f(-x)$, the function is odd. Any other situation indicates the function is neither even nor odd. To graphically determine if a function is even, odd, or neither, symmetry needs to be evaluated. If the function is perfectly symmetrical across the y-axis, it is an even function. If it is symmetrical about the origin, the function is odd. Any other situation indicates that the function is neither even nor odd.

It should be noted that there is one function that is both even *and* odd: $f(x) = 0$.

Polynomial Functions

A *polynomial function* is a function containing a polynomial expression, which is an expression containing constants and variables combined using the four mathematical operations. The degree of a polynomial in one variable is the largest exponent seen on any variable in the expression. Typical polynomial functions are *quartic*, with a degree of 4, *cubic*, with a degree of 3, and *quadratic*, with a degree of 2. Note that the exponents on the variables can only be nonnegative integers. The domain of any polynomial function is all real numbers because any number plugged into a polynomial expression grants a real number output. An example of a quartic polynomial equation is $y = x^4 + 3x^3 - 2x + 1$. The zeros of a polynomial function are the points where its graph crosses the y-axis. In order to find the number of real zeros of a polynomial function, *Descartes' Rule of Sign* can be used. The number of possible positive real zeros is equal to the number of sign changes in the coefficients of the terms in the polynomial. If there is only one sign change, there is only one positive real zero. In the example above, the signs of the coefficients are positive, positive, negative, and positive. Therefore, the sign changes two times and therefore, there are at most two positive real zeros. The number of possible negative real zeros is equal to the number of sign changes in the coefficients when plugging $-x$ into the equation. Again, if there is only one sign change, there is only one negative real zero. The polynomial result when plugging $-x$ into the equation is $y^4 - 3x^3 + 2x + 1$. The sign changes two times, so there are at most two negative real zeros. Another polynomial equation this rule can be applied to is $y = x^3 + 2x - x - 5$. There is only one sign change in the terms of the polynomial, so there is exactly one real zero. When plugging $-x$ into the equation, the polynomial result is $-x^3 - 2x - x - 5$. There are no sign changes in this polynomial, so there are no possible negative zeros.

Algebraic Functions

A *relation* is any set of ordered pairs (x, y). The first set of points, known as the *x*-coordinates, make up the domain of the relation. The second set of points, known as the *y*-coordinates, make up the range of the relation. A relation in which every member of the domain corresponds to only one member of the range is known as a *function*. A function cannot have a member of the domain corresponding to two members of the range. Functions are most often given in terms of equations instead of ordered pairs. For instance, here is an equation of a line: $y = 2x + 4$. In function notation, this can be written as $f(x) = 2x + 4$. The expression $f(x)$ is read "f of x" and it shows that the inputs, the *x*-values, get plugged into the function and the output is $y = f(x)$. The set of all inputs are in the domain and the set of all outputs are in the range.

The *x*-values are known as the *independent variables* of the function and the *y*-values are known as the *dependent variables* of the function. The *y*-values depend on the *x*-values. For instance, if $x = 2$ is plugged into the function shown above, the *y*-value depends on that input.

$$f(2) = 2 \times 2 + 4 = 8.$$

Therefore, $f(2) = 8$, which is the same as writing the ordered pair (2, 8). To graph a function, graph it in equation form. Therefore, replace $f(x)$ with h and plot ordered pairs.

Due to the definition of a function, the graph of a function cannot have two first components being paired to the same second component. Therefore, all graphs of functions pass the *vertical line test*. If any vertical line intersects a graph in more than one place, the graph is not that of a function. For example, the graph of a circle is not a function because one can draw a vertical line through a circle and it would intersect the circle twice. Common functions include lines and polynomials, and they all pass the vertical line test.

Piecewise Functions

A *piecewise function* is basically a function that is defined in pieces. The graph of the function behaves differently over different intervals along the *x*-axis, or different intervals of its domain. Therefore, the function is defined using different mathematical expressions over these intervals. The function is not defined by only one equation. In a piecewise function, the function is actually defined by two or more equations, where each equation is used over a specific interval of the domain.

Here is a graph of a piecewise function:

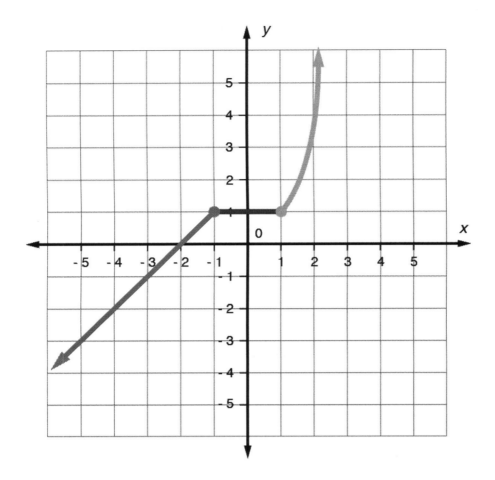

Notice that from $(-\infty, -1]$, the graph is a line with a positive slope. From $[-1, 1]$ the graph is a horizontal line. Finally, from $[1, \infty)$ the graph is a nonlinear curve. Both the domain and range of this piecewise defined function are all real numbers, which is expressed as $(-\infty, \infty)$.

Piecewise functions can also have discontinuities, which are jumps in the graph. When drawing a graph, if the pencil must be picked up at any point to continue drawing, the graph has a discontinuity.

Here is the graph of a piecewise function with discontinuities at $x = 1$ and $x = 2$:

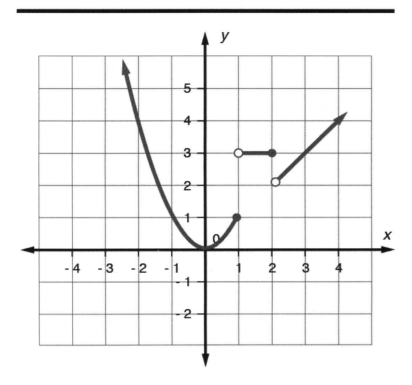

A Piecewise Function

The open circle at a point indicates that the endpoint is not included in that part of the graph, and the closed circle indicates that the endpoint is included. The domain of this function is all real numbers; however, the range is all nonnegative real numbers $[0, \infty)$.

Exponential Functions

Linear growth involves a quantity, the dependent variable, increasing or decreasing at a constant rate as another quantity, the independent variable, increases as well. The graph of linear growth is a straight line. Linear growth is represented as the following equation: $y = mx + b$, where m is the *slope* of the line, also known as the *rate of change*, and b is the y-intercept. If the y-intercept is 0, then the linear growth is actually known as direct variation. If the slope is positive, the dependent variable increases as the independent variable increases, and if the slope is negative, the dependent variable decreases as the independent variable increases.

Exponential growth involves a quantity, the dependent variable, changing by a common ratio every unit increase or equal interval. The equation of exponential growth is $y = a^x$ for $a > 0, a \neq 1$. The value a is known as the *base*. Consider the exponential equation $y = 2^x$. When $x = 1$, $y = 2$, and when $x = 2$, $y = 4$. For every unit increase in x, the value of the output variable doubles. Here is the graph of $y = 2^x$. Notice that as the dependent variable, y, gets very large, x increases slightly. This characteristic of the graph is sometimes why a quantity is said to be blowing up exponentially.

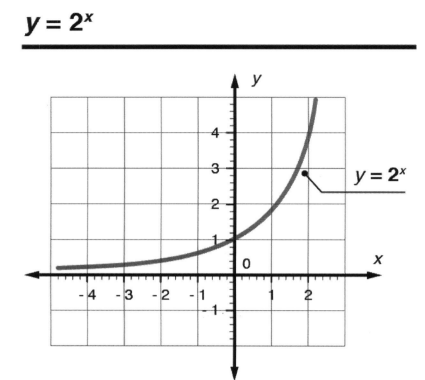

$$y = 2^x$$

Radical Functions

Recall that a *radical expression* is an expression involving a square root, a cube root, or a higher order root such as fourth root, fifth root, etc. The expression underneath the radical is known as the radicand, and the index is the number corresponding to the root. An index of 2 corresponds to a square root. A radical function is a function that involves a radical expression. For example, $\sqrt{x+1}$ is a radical expression, $x + 1$ is the radicand, and the corresponding function is $y = \sqrt{x+1}$. The function can also be written in function notation as $f(x) = \sqrt{x+1}$. If the root is even, meaning a square root, fourth root, etc., the radicand must be positive. Therefore, in order to find the domain of a radical function with an even index, set the radicand greater than or equal to zero and find the set of numbers that satisfies that inequality. The domain of $f(x) = \sqrt{x+1}$ is all numbers greater than or equal to -1. The range of this function is all nonnegative real numbers because the square root, or any even root, can never output a negative number. The domain of an odd root is all real numbers because the radicand can be negative in an odd root.

Logarithmic Functions

For $x > 0$, $b > 0$, $b \neq 1$, the function $f(x) = \log_b x$ is known as the *logarithmic function* with base b. With $y = \log_b x$, its exponential equivalent is $b^y = x$. In either case, the exponent is y and the base is b. Therefore, $3 = \log_2 8$ is the same as $2^2 = 8$. So, in order to find the logarithm with base 2 of 8, find the exponent that when 2 is raised to that value results in 8. Similarly, $\log_3 243 = 5$. In order to do this mentally, ask the question, what exponent does 3 need to be raised to that results in 234? The answer is 5. Most logarithms do not have whole number results. In this case, a calculator can be used. A calculator typically has buttons with base 10 and base e, so the change of base formula can be used to calculate these logs. For instance, $\log_3 55 = \frac{\log 55}{\log 3} = 3.64$. Similarly, the natural logarithm with base e could be used to obtain the same result. $\log_3 55 = \frac{\ln 55}{\ln 3} = 3.64$.

The domain of a logarithmic function $f(x) = \log_b x$ is all positive real numbers. This is because the exponent must be a positive number. The range of a logarithmic function $f(x) = \log_b x$ is all real numbers. The graphs of all logarithmic functions of the form $f(x) = \log_b x$ always pass through the point (1, 0) because anything raised to the power of 0 is 1. Therefore, such a function always has an x-intercept at 1. If the base is greater than 1, the graph increases from the left to the right along the x-axis. If the base is between 0 and 1, the graph decreases from the left to the right along the x-axis. In both situations, the y-axis is a vertical asymptote. The graph will never touch the y-axis, but it does approach it closely. Here are the graphs of the two cases of logarithmic functions:

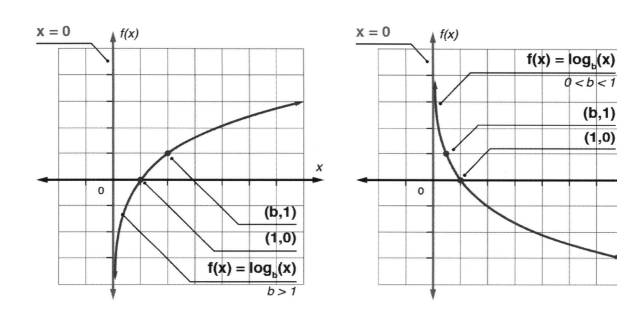

Trigonometric Functions

Within right triangles, trigonometric ratios can be defined for the acute angle within the triangle. Consider the following right triangle. The side across from the right angle is known as the *hypotenuse*, the acute angle being discussed is labeled θ, the side across from the acute angle is known as the *opposite* side, and the other side is known as the *adjacent* side.

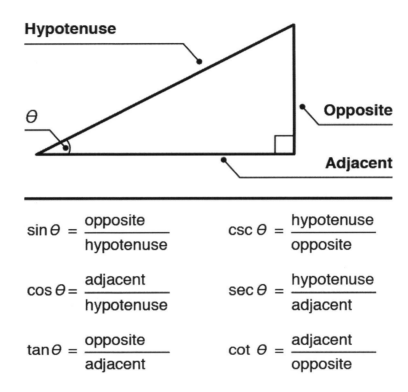

$$\sin\theta = \frac{\text{opposite}}{\text{hypotenuse}} \qquad \csc\theta = \frac{\text{hypotenuse}}{\text{opposite}}$$

$$\cos\theta = \frac{\text{adjacent}}{\text{hypotenuse}} \qquad \sec\theta = \frac{\text{hypotenuse}}{\text{adjacent}}$$

$$\tan\theta = \frac{\text{opposite}}{\text{adjacent}} \qquad \cot\theta = \frac{\text{adjacent}}{\text{opposite}}$$

The six trigonometric ratios are shown above as well. "Sin" is short for sine, "cos" is short for cosine, "tan" is short for tangent, "csc" is short for cosecant, "sec" is short for secant, and "cot" is short for cotangent. A mnemonic device exists that is helpful to remember the ratios. SOHCAHTOA stands for Sine = Opposite/Hypotenuse, Cosine = Adjacent/Hypotenuse, and Tangent = Opposite/Adjacent. The other three trigonometric ratios are reciprocals of sine, cosine, and tangent because $\csc\theta = \frac{1}{\sin\theta}$, $\sec\theta = \frac{1}{\cos\theta}$, and $\cot\theta = \frac{1}{\tan\theta}$.

The *Pythagorean Theorem* is an important relationship between the three sides of a right triangle. It states that the square of hypotenuse is equal to the sum of the squares of the other two sides. When using the Pythagorean Theorem, the hypotenuse is labeled as side c, the opposite is labeled as side a, and the adjacent side is side b. The theorem can be seen in the following diagram:

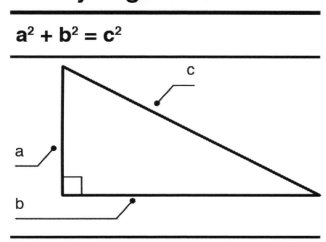

The Pythagorean Theorum

$$a^2 + b^2 = c^2$$

Both the trigonometric ratios and Pythagorean Theorem can be used in problems that involve finding either a missing side or missing angle of a right triangle. Look to see what sides and angles are given and select the correct relationship that will assist in finding the missing value. These relationships can also be used to solve application problems involving right triangles. Often, it is helpful to draw a figure to represent the problem to see what is missing.

Using the Relationship Between Similarity, Right Triangles, and Trigonometric Ratios
Within two similar triangles, corresponding side lengths are proportional, and angles are equal. In other words, regarding corresponding sides in two similar triangles, the ratio of side lengths is the same. Recall that the SAS theorem for similarity states that if an angle in one triangle is congruent to an angle in a second triangle, and the lengths of the sides in both triangles are proportional, then the triangles are similar. Also, because the ratio of two sides in two similar right triangles is the same, the trigonometric ratios in similar right triangles are always going to be equal.

If two triangles are similar, and one is a right triangle, the other is a right triangle. The definition of similarity ensures that each triangle has a 90-degree angle. In a similar sense, if two triangles are right triangles containing a pair of equal acute angles, the triangles are similar because the third pair of angles must be equal as well. However, right triangles are not necessarily always similar.

The following triangles are similar:

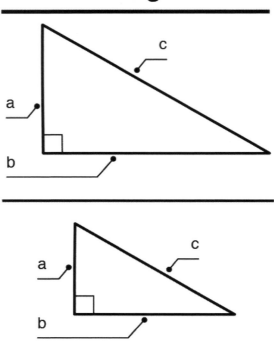

Similar Triangles

It is not apparent at first glance; however, theorems can be used to show similarity. The Pythagorean Theorem can be used to find the missing side lengths in both triangles. In the larger triangle, the missing side is the hypotenuse, c. Therefore, $9^2 + 12^2 = c^2$. This equation is equivalent to $225 = c^2$, so taking the square root of both sides results in the positive root $c = 15$. In the other triangle, the Pythagorean theorem can be used to find the missing side length b. The theorem shows that $6^2 + b^2 = 10^2$, and b is then solved for to obtain $b = 8$. The ratio of the sides in the larger triangle to the sides in the smaller triangle is the same value, 1.5. Therefore, the sides are proportional. Because they are both right triangles, they have a congruent angle. The SAS theorem for similarity can be used to show that these two triangles are similar.

Using the Relationship Between Sine and Cosine of Complementary Angles
Two *complementary angles* add up to 90 degrees, or π radians. Within a right triangle, the sine of an angle is equal to the ratio of the side opposite the angle to the hypotenuse and the cosine of an angle is equal to the ratio of the side adjacent to the angle to the hypotenuse. Within a right triangle, there is a right angle, and because the sum of all angles in a triangle is 180 degrees, the two other angles add up to

90 degrees, and are therefore complementary. Consider the following right triangle with angles A, B, and C, and sides a, b, and c.

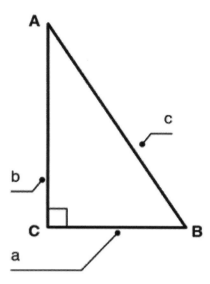

It is true by using such ratios described above that $\sin B = \frac{b}{c}$ and $\cos B = \frac{a}{c}$. Also, it is true that $\cos A = \frac{b}{c}$ and $\sin A = \frac{a}{c}$. Therefore, $\sin B = \cos A$ and $\cos B = \sin A$. A and B are complementary angles, so given two complementary angles, the sine of one equals the cosine of the other, and the cosine of one equals the sine of the other. Given the two complementary angles 30 degrees and 60 degrees, $\sin 30 = \frac{1}{2}$, $\cos 60 = \frac{1}{2}$, $\cos 30 = \frac{\sqrt{3}}{2}$, and $\sin 60 = \frac{\sqrt{3}}{2}$. Either a calculator set in degrees mode, a unit circle, or the Pythagorean Theorem could be used to find all of these values.

Using Trigonometric Functions of Radian Measure
When inputting values into trigonometric functions, the values can either be in degrees or radians. It is important when using calculators to evaluate trigonometric functions that the calculator is in the correct mode: degrees or radians. If a calculator is in the mode in which it is supposed to use degrees, and a value in radians is plugged into a trig function, the result will be incorrect.

Another way to evaluate trig functions in degrees and radians is to use the *unit circle*. When using radians, the degree measure used should be the one in radians, which would contain a multiple of π. Here is a unit circle:

The Unit Circle

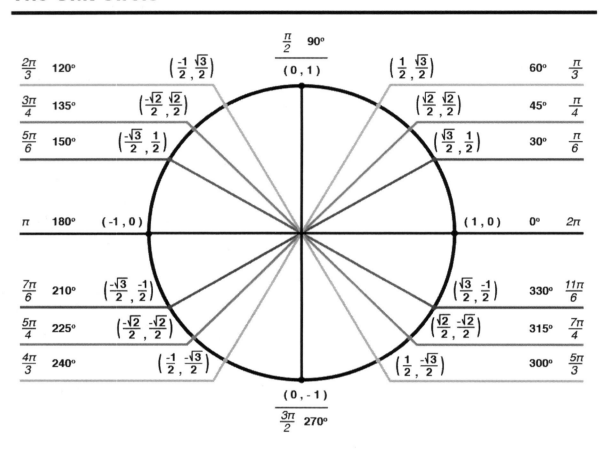

Notice that each angle measure is given in both radians and degrees. The *sine* of an angle is the *y*-coordinate of the corresponding ordered pair. For instance, $\sin \pi = 0$. The *cosine* of any angle is the *x*-coordinate of the corresponding ordered pair, and therefore, $\cos \pi = -1$. The *tangent* of any angle is the ratio of the *y*-coordinate over the *x*-coordinate, and therefore $\tan \pi = \frac{0}{-1} = 0$. *Cosecant, secant,* and *cotangent* of any angles are the corresponding reciprocals of sine, cosine, and tangent. In this case, $\csc \pi$ is undefined, $\sec \pi = -1$, and $\cot \pi$ is undefined.

Practice Questions

1. Which of the following relations is a function?
   a. {(1, 4), (1, 3), (2, 4), (5, 6)}
   b. {(-1, -1), (-2, -2), (-3, -3), (-4, -4)}
   c. {(0, 0), (1, 0), (2, 0), (1, 1)}
   d. {(1, 0), (1, 2), (1, 3), (1, 4)}
   e. {(-1, 6), (2, 12), (8, 34), (-1, 42)}

2. Find the indicated function value: $f(5)$ for $f(x) = x^2 - 2x + 1$.
   a. 16
   b. 1
   c. 5
   d. -8
   e. -2

3. What is the domain of $f(x) = 4x^2 + 2x - 1$?
   a. $(0, \infty)$
   b. $(-\infty, 0)$
   c. $(-64, 64)$
   d. $(-1, 4)$
   e. $(-\infty, \infty)$

4. The function $f(x) = 3.1x + 240$ models the total U.S. population, in millions, x years after the year 1980. Use this function to answer the following question: What is the total U.S. population in 2011? Round to the nearest million.
   a. 336 people
   b. 336 million people
   c. 6,474 people
   d. 647 million people
   e. 6.474 million people

5. What is the domain of the logarithmic function $f(x) = \log_2(x - 2)$?
   a. 2
   b. $(-\infty, \infty)$
   c. $(0, \infty)$
   d. $(2, \infty)$
   e. $(-2, \infty)$

6. The function $f(t) = \frac{20,000}{1+10e^{-2t}}$ represents the number of people who catch a disease t weeks after its initial outbreak in a population of 20,000 people. How many people initially had the disease at the time of the initial outbreak? Round to the nearest whole number.
   a. 20,000
   b. 1,818
   c. 2,000
   d. 0
   e. 18,000

7. What are the zeros of the following quadratic function?
$$f(x) = 2x^2 - 12x + 16$$

    a. $x = 2$ and $x = 4$
    b. $x = 8$ and $x = 2$
    c. $x = 2$ and $x = 0$
    d. $x = 0$ and $x = 4$
    e. $x = -2$ and $x = 2$

8. What is the equivalent exponential form of the following logarithmic function?
$$f(x) = \log_5(x + 3)$$

    a. $3^y = x$
    b. $5^y = x$
    c. $5^{(x+3)} = y$
    d. $3^y = x + 5$
    e. $5^y = x + 3$

9. What is the range of the polynomial function $f(x) = 2x^2 + 5$?
    a. $(-\infty, \infty)$
    b. $(2, \infty)$
    c. $(0, \infty)$
    d. $[5, \infty)$
    e. $[1, \infty)$

10. What is an equivalent logarithmic form of the following exponential function?
$$f(x) = 10^{x+3}$$

    a. $x = 3 + \log y$
    b. $-3 + \log y = x$
    c. $\log(x - 3) = y$
    d. $\log_3 x = y$
    e. $3 + \log y = 3x$

11. For which two values of x is $g(x) = 4x + 4$ equal to $g(x) = x^2 + 3x + 2$?
    a. 1, 0
    b. 2, -1
    c. 0, 2
    d. 1, 2
    e. -1, 2

12. The population of coyotes in the local national forest has been declining since 2000. The population can be modeled by the function $y = -(x - 2)^2 + 1600$, where y represents number of coyotes and x represents the number of years past 2000. When will there be no more coyotes?
    a. 2020
    b. 2040
    c. 2012
    d. 2042
    e. 2036

13. Given the linear function $g(x) = \frac{1}{4}x - 2$, which domain value corresponds to a range value of $\frac{1}{8}$?

    a. $\frac{17}{2}$

    b. $-\frac{63}{32}$

    c. 0

    d. $\frac{2}{17}$

    e. $\frac{63}{32}$

14. A ball is thrown up from a building that is 800 feet high. Its position s in feet above the ground is given by the function $s = -32t^2 + 90t + 800$, where t is the number of seconds since the ball was thrown. How long will it take for the ball to come back to its starting point? Round your answer to the nearest tenth of a second.

    a. 0 seconds
    b. 2.8 seconds
    c. 3 seconds
    d. 8 seconds
    e. 5.6 seconds

15. What are the zeros of the following cubic function?
$$g(x) = x^3 - 2x^2 - 9x + 18$$

    a. 2, 3
    b. 2, 3, -2
    c. 2, 3, -3
    d. 2, -2
    e. -2, 3, -3

16. What is the domain of the following rational function?
$$f(x) = \frac{x^3 + 2x + 1}{2 - x}$$

    a. $(-\infty, -2) \cup (-2, \infty)$
    b. $(-\infty, 2) \cup (2, \infty)$
    c. $(2, \infty)$
    d. $(-2, \infty)$
    e. $(-\infty, 1) \cup (1, \infty)$

17. Given the function $f(x) = 4x - 2$, what is the correct form of the simplified difference quotient:
$$\frac{f(x + h) - f(x)}{h}$$

    a. $4x - 1$
    b. $4x$
    c. 4
    d. $4x + h$
    e. $4x + 1$

18. Determine whether the function $g(x) = 7x^3 + 5x - 2$ is odd, even, both even and odd, or neither even nor odd.
- a. Odd
- b. Even
- c. Both
- d. Neither
- e. Cannot be determined

19. The mass of the moon is about 7.348×10^{22} kilograms and the mass of Earth is 5.972×10^{24} kilograms. How many times GREATER is Earth's mass than the moon's mass?
- a. 8.127×10^1
- b. 8.127
- c. 812.7
- d. 8.127×10^{-1}
- e. 8.127×10^{-2}

20. What is the equation of the line that passes through the two points (-3, 7) and (-1, -5)?
- a. $y = 6x + 11$
- b. $y = 6x$
- c. $y = 6x - 11$
- d. $y = -6x$
- e. $y = -6x - 11$

21. The percentage of smokers above the age of 18 in 2000 was 23.2 percent. The percentage of smokers above the age of 18 in 2015 was 15.1 percent. Find the average rate of change in the percent of smokers above the age of 18 from 2000 to 2015.
- a. -.54 percent
- b. -54 percent
- c. -5.4 percent
- d. -15 percent
- e. -1.5 percent

22. In order to estimate deer population in a forest, biologists obtained a sample of deer in that forest and tagged each one of them. The sample had 300 deer in total. They returned a week later and harmlessly captured 400 deer, and 5 were tagged. Use this information to estimate how many total deer were in the forest.
- a. 24,000 deer
- b. 30,000 deer
- c. 40,000 deer
- d. 80,000 deer
- e. 100,000 deer

23. The number of members of the House of Representatives varies directly with the total population in a state. If the state of New York has 20,000,000 residents and has 27 total representatives, how many should Ohio have with a population of 11,600,000?

    a. 10
    b. 16
    c. 11
    d. 5
    e. 8

24. What is the solution to the following system of linear equations?
$$2x + y = 14$$
$$4x + 2y = -28$$

    a. (0, 0)
    b. (14, -28)
    c. (2, -4)
    d. All real numbers
    e. There is no solution

25. Which of the following is perpendicular to the line $4x + 7y = 23$?

    a. $y = -\frac{4}{7}x + 23$
    b. $y = \frac{7}{4}x - 12$
    c. $4x + 7y = 14$
    d. $y = -\frac{7}{4}x + 11$
    e. $y = -\frac{7}{4}x + 12$

26. What is the solution to the following system of equations?
$$2x - y = 6$$
$$y = 8x$$

    a. (1, 8)
    b. (-1, 8)
    c. (-1, -8)
    d. All real numbers.
    e. There is no solution.

27. Which of the following is the equation of a vertical line that runs through the point (1, 4)?

    a. $x = 1$
    b. $y = 1$
    c. $x = 4$
    d. $y = 4$
    e. $x = -1$

28. What is the missing length x?

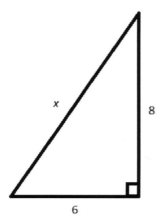

  a. 6
  b. -10
  c. 10
  d. 100
  e. 8

29. What is the correct factorization of the following binomial?
$$2y^3 - 128$$

  a. $2(y + 8)(y - 8)$
  b. $2(y - 4)(y^2 + 4y + 16)$
  c. $2(y - 4)(y + 4)^2$
  d. $2(y - 4)^3$
  e. $2(y + 4)(y^2 - 4y)$

Answer Explanations

1. B: The only relation in which every x-value corresponds to exactly one y-value is the relation given in B, making it a function. The other relations have the same first component paired up to different second components, which goes against the definition of functions.

2. A: To find a function value, plug in the number given for the variable and evaluate the expression, using the order of operations (parentheses, exponents, multiplication, division, addition, subtraction). The function given is a polynomial function and $f(5) = 5^2 - 2 \times 5 + 1 = 25 - 10 + 1 = 16$.

3. E: The function given is a polynomial function. Anything can be plugged into a polynomial function to get an output. Therefore, its domain is all real numbers, which is expressed in interval notation as $(-\infty, \infty)$.

4. B: The variable x represents the number of years after 1980. The year 2011 was 31 years after 1980, so plug 31 into the function to obtain $f(31) = 3.1 \times 31 + 240 = 336.1$. This value rounds to 336 and represents 336 million people.

5. D: The argument of a logarithmic function has to be greater than or equal to zero. Basically, one cannot take the logarithm of a negative number or 0. Therefore, to find the domain, set the argument greater than 0 and solve the inequality. This results in $x - 2 > 0$, or $x > 2$. Therefore, in order to obtain an output of the function, the number plugged into the function must be greater than 2. This domain is represented as $(2, \infty)$.

6. B: The time of the initial outbreak corresponds to $t = 0$. Therefore, 0 must be plugged into the function. This results in $\frac{20{,}000}{1+10e^0} = \frac{20{,}000}{1+10} = \frac{20{,}000}{11} = 1{,}818.182$, which rounds to 1,818. Therefore, there were 1,818 people in the population that initially had the disease.

7. A: The zeros of a polynomial function are the x-values where the graph crosses the x-axis, or where $y = 0$. Therefore, set $y = 0$ and solve the polynomial equation. This quadratic can be solved using factoring, as follows:

$$0 = 2x^2 - 12x + 16 = 2(x^2 - 6x + 8) = 2(x - 4)(x - 2).$$

Setting both factors equal to 0 results in the two solutions $x = 4$ and $x = 2$, which are the zeros of the original function.

8. E: Given a logarithmic function $f(x) = \log_b x$, its base is b and it can be written as $y = \log_b x$ with equivalent exponential equation $b^y = x$. In this problem, the base is 5, so its equivalent exponential equation is $5^y = x + 3$.

9. D: This is a parabola that opens up, as the coefficient on the x^2 term is positive. The smallest number in its range occurs when plugging 0 into the function $f(0) = 5$. Any other output is a number larger than 5, even when a positive number is plugged in. When a negative number gets plugged into the function, the output is positive, and same with a positive number. Therefore, the domain is written as $[5, \infty)$ in interval notation.

10. B: The equivalent equation form of the function is $y = 10^{x+3}$, with base 10. The expression can be written in logarithmic form as $\log_{10} y = x + 3$. A logarithm with base 10 is known as the common logarithm and is written without the base. Adding -3 to both sides results in $-3 + \log y = x$.

11. E: First set the functions equal to one another, resulting in $x^2 + 3x + 2 = 4x + 4$. This is a quadratic equation, so the equivalent equation in standard form is $x^2 - x - 2 = 0$. This equation can be solved by factoring into $(x - 2)(x + 1) = 0$. Setting both factors equal to zero results in $x = 2$ and $x = -1$.

12. D: There will be no more coyotes when the population is 0, so set y equal to 0 and solve the quadratic equation $0 = -(x - 2)^2 + 1600$. Subtract 1600 from both sides and divide through by -1. This results in $1600 = (x - 2)^2$. Then, take the square root of both sides. This process results in the following equation: $\pm 40 = x - 2$. Adding 2 to both sides results in two solutions: $x = 42$ and $x = -38$. Because the problem involves years after 2000, the only solution that makes sense is 42. Add 42 to 2000, so therefore in 2042 there will be no more coyotes.

13. A: The range value is given, and this is the output of the function. Therefore, the function must be set equal to $\frac{1}{8}$ and solved for x. Thus, $\frac{1}{8} = \frac{1}{4}x - 2$ needs to be solved. The fractions can be cleared by multiplying times the LCD 8. This results in $1 = 2x - 16$. Add 16 to both sides and divide by 2 to obtain $x = \frac{17}{2}$.

14. B: The ball is back at the starting point when the function is equal to 800 feet. Therefore, this results in solving the equation $800 = -32t^2 + 90t + 800$. Subtract 800 off of both sides and factor the remaining terms to obtain $0 = 2t(-16 + 45t)$. Setting both factors equal to 0 result in $t = 0$, which is when the ball was thrown up initially, and $t = \frac{45}{16} = 2.8$ seconds. Therefore, it will take the ball 2.8 seconds to come back down to its staring point.

15. C: To find the zeros, set the function equal to 0 and factor the polynomial. Because there are four terms, it should be factored by grouping. Factor a common factor out of the first set of two terms, and then find a shared binomial factor in the second set of two terms. This results in $x^2(x - 2) - 9(x - 2) = 0$. The binomial can then be factored out of each set to get $(x^2 - 9)(x - 2) = 0$. This can be factored further as $(x + 3)(x - 3)(x - 2) = 0$. Setting each factor equal to zero and solving results in the three zeros -3, 3, and 2.

16. B: Given a rational function, the expression in the denominator can never be equal to 0. To find the domain, set the denominator equal to 0 and solve for x. This results in $2 - x = 0$, and its solution is $x = 2$. This value needs to be excluded from the set of all real numbers, and therefore the domain written in interval notation is $(-\infty, 2) \cup (2, \infty)$.

17. C: Plugging the function into the formula results in:

$$\frac{4(x + h) - 2 - (4x - 2)}{h}$$

which is simplified to:

$$\frac{4x + 4h - 2 - 4x + 2}{h} = \frac{4h}{h} = h$$

This value is also equal to the derivative of the given function. The derivative of a linear function is its slope.

18. D: To determine whether a function is even or odd, plug $-x$ into the function. If the result is $f(x)$ the function is even, and if the result is $-f(x)$ the function is odd.

$$g(-x) = 7(-x)^3 + 5(-x) - 2 = -7x^3 - 5x - 2$$

This function is neither $f(x)$ nor $-f(x)$, so the given function is neither even nor odd.

19. A: Division can be used to solve this problem. The division necessary is:

$$\frac{5.972 \times 10^{24}}{7.348 \times 10^{22}}$$

To compute this division, divide the constants first then use algebraic laws of exponents to divide the exponential expression. This results in about 0.8127×10^2, which written in scientific notation is 8.127×10^1.

20. E: First, the slope of the line must be found. This is equal to the change in y over the change in x, given the two points. Therefore, the slope is -6. The slope and one of the points are then plugged into the slope-intercept form of a line: $y - y_1 = m(x - x_1)$. This results in $y - 7 = -6(x + 3)$. The -6 is simplified and the equation is solved for y to obtain $y = -6x - 11$.

21. A: The formula for the rate of change is the same as slope: change in y over change in x. The y-value in this case is percentage of smokers and the x-value is year. The change in percentage of smokers from 2000 to 2015 was 8.1 percent. The change in x was $2000 - 2015 = -15$. Therefore, $\frac{8.1\%}{-15} = -0.54\%$. The percentage of smokers decreased 0.54 percent each year.

22. A: A proportion should be used to solve this problem. The ratio of tagged to total deer in each instance is set equal, and the unknown quantity is a variable x. The proportion is $\frac{300}{x} = \frac{5}{400}$. Cross-multiplying gives $120,000 = 5x$, and dividing through by 5 results in 24,000.

23. B: The number of representatives varies directly with the population, so the equation necessary is $N = k \times P$, where N is number of representatives, k is the variation constant, and P is total population in millions. Plugging in the information for New York allows k to be solved for. This process gives $27 = k \times 20$, so $k = 1.35$. Therefore, the formula for number of representatives given total population in millions is $N = 1.35 \times P$. Plugging in $P = 11.6$ for Ohio results in $N = 15.66$, which rounds up to 16 total Representatives.

24. E: This system can be solved using the method of substitution. Solving the first equation for y results in $y = 14 - 2x$. Plugging this into the second equation gives $4x + 2(14 - 2x) = -28$, which simplifies to $28 = -28$, an untrue statement. Therefore, this system has no solution because no x value will satisfy the system.

25. B: The slopes of perpendicular lines are negative reciprocals, meaning their product is equal to -1. The slope of the line given needs to be found. Its equivalent form in slope-intercept form is $y = -\frac{4}{7}x + 23$, so its slope is $-\frac{4}{7}$. The negative reciprocal of this number is $\frac{7}{4}$. The only line in the options given with this same slope is $y = \frac{7}{4}x - 12$.

26. C: This system can be solved using substitution. Plug the second equation in for y in the first equation to obtain $2x - 8x = 6$, which simplifies to $-6x = 6$. Divide both sides by 6 to get $x = -1$, which is then back-substituted into either original equation to obtain $y = -8$.

27. A: A vertical line has the same x value for any point on the line. Other points on the line would be (1, 3), (1, 5), (1, 9,) etc. Mathematically, this is written as $x = 1$. A vertical line is always of the form $x = a$ for some constant a.

28. C: The Pythagorean Theorem can be used to find the missing length x because it is a right triangle. The theorem states that $6^2 + 8^2 = x^2$, which simplifies into $100 = x^2$. Taking the positive square root of both sides results in the missing value $x = 10$.

29. B: First, the common factor 2 can be factored out of both terms, resulting in $2(y^3 - 64)$. The resulting binomial is a difference of cubes that can be factored using the rule $a^3 - b^3 = (a - b)(a^2 + ab + b^2)$ with a = y and b = 4. Therefore, the result is $2(y - 4)(y^2 + 4y + 16)$.

Elementary Algebra

Operations with Integers and Rational Numbers

Computation with Integers and Negative Rational Numbers

Rational numbers are any numbers that can be written as a fraction of integers. Operations to be performed on rational numbers include adding, subtracting, multiplying, and dividing. Essentially, this refers to performing these operations on fractions. Adding and subtracting fractions must be completed by first finding the least common denominator. For example, the problem $\frac{3}{5} + \frac{6}{7}$ requires that the common multiple be found between 5 and 7. The smallest number that divides evenly by 5 and 7 is 35. For the denominators to become 35, they must be multiplied by 7 and 5 respectively. The fraction $\frac{3}{5}$ can be multiplied by 7 on the top and bottom to yield the fraction $\frac{21}{35}$. The fraction $\frac{6}{7}$ can be multiplied by 5 to yield the fraction $\frac{30}{35}$. Now that the fractions have the same denominator, the numerators can be added. The answer to the addition problem becomes $\frac{3}{5} + \frac{6}{7} = \frac{21}{35} + \frac{30}{35} = \frac{41}{35}$. The same technique can be used for subtraction of rational numbers. The operations multiplication and division may seem easier to perform because finding common denominators is unnecessary. If the problem reads $\frac{1}{3} \times \frac{4}{5}$, then the numerators and denominators are multiplied by each other and the answer is found to be $\frac{4}{15}$. For division, the problem must be changed to multiplication before performing operations. The following words can be used to remember to leave, change, and flip before multiplying. If the problem reads $\frac{3}{7} \div \frac{3}{4}$, then the first fraction is *left* alone, the operation is *changed* to multiplication, and then the last fraction is *flipped*. The problem becomes $\frac{3}{7} \times \frac{4}{3} = \frac{12}{21}$.

Other rational numbers include negative numbers, where two may be added. When two negative numbers are added, the result is a negative number with an even greater magnitude. When a negative number is added to a positive number, the result depends on the value of each addend. For example, $-4 + 8 = 4$ because the positive number is larger than the negative number. For multiplying two negative numbers, the result is positive. For example, $-4 \times -3 = 12$, where the negatives cancel out and yield a positive answer.

Rational numbers can be whole or negative numbers, fractions, or repeating decimals because these numbers can all be written as a fraction. Whole numbers can be written as fractions, where 25 and 17 can be written as $\frac{25}{1}$ and $\frac{17}{1}$. One way of interpreting these fractions is to say that they are *ratios*, or comparisons of two quantities. The fractions given may represent 25 students to 1 classroom, or 17 desks to 1 computer lab. Repeating decimals can also be written as fractions of integers, such as 0.3333 and 0.6666667. These repeating decimals can be written as the fractions $\frac{1}{3}$ and $\frac{2}{3}$. Fractions can be described as having a part-to-whole relationship. The $\frac{1}{3}$ may represent 1 piece of pizza out of the whole cut into 3 pieces. The fraction $\frac{2}{3}$ may represent 2 pieces of the same whole pizza. One operation to perform on rational numbers, or fractions, can be addition. Adding the fractions $\frac{1}{3}$ and $\frac{2}{3}$ can be as simple as adding the numerators, 1 and 2. Because the denominator on both fractions is 3, that means the parts on the top have the same meaning or are the same size piece of pizza. When adding these fractions, the result is $\frac{3}{3}$, or 1. Both of these numbers are rational and represent a whole, or in this problem, a whole pizza.

Other than fractions, rational numbers also include whole numbers and negative integers. When whole numbers are added, other than zero, the result is always greater than the addends. For example, the equation $4 + 18 = 22$ shows 4 increased by 18, with a result of 22. When subtracting rational numbers, sometimes the result is a negative number. For example, the equation $5 - 12 = -7$ shows that taking 12 away from 5 results in a negative answer because 5 is smaller than 12. The difference is -7 because the starting number is smaller than the number taken away. For multiplication and division, similar results are found. Multiplying rational numbers may look like the following equation: $5 \times 7 = 35$, where both numbers are positive and whole, and the result is a larger number than the factors. The number 5 is counted 7 times, which results in a total of 35. Sometimes, the equation looks like $-4 \times 3 = -12$, so the result is negative because a positive number times a negative number gives a negative answer. The rule is that any time a negative number and a positive number are multiplied or divided, the result is negative.

The Use of Absolute Values

The *absolute value* of any real number is the distance from that number to 0 on the number line. The absolute value of a number can never be negative. For example, the absolute value of both 8 and -8 is 8 because they are both 8 units away from 0 on the number line. This is written as $|8| = |-8| = 8$.

Ordering

Ordering rational numbers is a way to compare two or more different numerical values. Determining whether two amounts are equal, less than, or greater than is the basis for comparing both positive and negative numbers. Also, a group of numbers can be compared by ordering them from the smallest amount to the largest amount. A few symbols are necessary to use when ordering rational numbers. The equals sign, $=$, shows that the two quantities on either side of the symbol have the same value. For example, $\frac{12}{3} = 4$ because both values are equivalent. Another symbol that is used to compare numbers is $<$, which represents "less than." With this symbol, the smaller number is placed on the left and the larger number is placed on the right. Always remember that the symbol's "mouth" opens up to the larger number. When comparing negative and positive numbers, it is important to remember that the number occurring to the left on the number line is always smaller and is placed to the left of the symbol. This idea might seem confusing because some values could appear at first glance to be larger, even though they are not. For example, $-5 < 4$ is read as "negative 5 is less than 4." Here is an image of a number line for help:

The symbol $\leq$ represents "less than or equal to," and it joins $<$ with equality. Therefore, both $-5 \leq 4$ and $-5 \leq -5$ are true statements, and "-5 is less than or equal to both 4 and -5." Other symbols are $>$ and $\geq$, which represent "greater than" and "greater than or equal to." Both $4 \geq -1$ and $-1 \geq -1$ are correct ways to use these symbols.

Here is a chart of these four inequality symbols:

Symbol	Definition
$<$	less than
$\leq$	less than or equal to
$>$	greater than
$\geq$	greater than or equal to

Comparing integers is a straightforward process, especially when using the number line, but the comparison of decimals and fractions is not as obvious. When comparing two non-negative decimals, compare digit by digit, starting from the left. The larger value contains the first larger digit. For example, 0.1456 is larger than 0.1234 because the value 4 in the hundredths place in the first decimal is larger than the value 2 in the hundredths place in the second decimal. When comparing a fraction with a decimal, convert the fraction to a decimal and then compare in the same manner. Finally, there are a few options when comparing fractions. If two non-negative fractions have the same denominator, the fraction with the larger numerator is the larger value. If they have different denominators, they can be converted to equivalent fractions with a common denominator to be compared, or they can be converted to decimals to be compared. When comparing two negative decimals or fractions, a different approach must be used. It is important to remember that the smaller number exists to the left on the number line. Therefore, when comparing two negative decimals by place value, the number with the larger first place value is smaller due to the negative sign. Whichever value is closer to 0 is larger. For instance, -0.456 is larger than -0.498 because of the values in the hundredth places. If two negative fractions have the same denominator, the fraction with the larger numerator is smaller because of the negative sign.

Operations with Algebraic Expressions

Evaluating Simple Formulas and Expressions

Given the formula for the area of a rectangle $A = lw$, with A = area, l = length, and w = width, the area of a rectangle can be determined, given the length and the width.

For example, if the length of a rectangle is 7 cm and the width is 10 cm, find the area of the rectangle.

Solution: Just as when evaluating expressions, replace the variables with the given values.

Given $A = lw$, $l = 7$ and $w = 10$.

$A = (7)(10)$ Replace l with 7 and w with 10

$A = 70$ Multiply

Therefore, the area of the rectangle is 70 cm^2.

Example: The formula for perimeter of a rectangle, $P = 2l + 2w$, where P is perimeter, l is length, and w is width. If the length of a rectangle is 12 inches and the width is 9 inches, find the perimeter.

Solution: $P = 2l + 2w$

$P = 2(12) + 2(9)$ Replace l with 12 and w with 9

$P = 24 + 18$ Use correct order of operations; multiply first

$P = 42$ Add

The perimeter of this rectangle is 42 inches.

Independent variables are independent, meaning they are not changed by other variables within the context of the problem. *Dependent variables* are dependent, meaning they may change depending on how other variables change in the problem. For example, in the formula for the perimeter of a fence, the length and width are the independent variables and the perimeter is the dependent variable. The formula is shown below.

$$P = 2l + 2w$$

As the width or the length changes, the perimeter may also change. The first variables to change are the length and width, which then result in a change in perimeter. The change does not come first with the perimeter and then with length and width. When comparing these two types of variables, it is helpful to ask which variable causes the change and which variable is affected by the change.

Another formula to represent this relationship is the formula for circumference show below.

$$C = \pi \times d$$

The C represents circumference and the d represents diameter. The pi symbol represents the ratio $\frac{22}{7}$ or approximately 3.14. In this formula, the diameter of the circle is the independent variable. It is the portion of the circle that changes, therefore changing the circumference as a result. The circumference is the variable that is being changed by the diameter, so it is called the dependent variable. It depends on the value of the diameter.

Another place to recognize independent and dependent variables can be in experiments. A common experiment is one where the growth of a plant is tested based on the amount of sunlight it receives. Each plant in the experiment is given a different amount of sunlight, but the same amount of other nutrients like light and water. The growth of the plants is measured over a given time period and the results show how much sunlight is best for plants. In this experiment, the independent variable is the amount of sunlight that each plant receives. The dependent variable is the growth of each plant. The growth depends on the amount of sunlight, which gives reason for the distinction between independent and dependent variables.

Adding and Subtracting Monomials and Polynomials

When working with polynomials, *like terms* are terms that contain exactly the same variables with the same powers. For example, x^4y^5 and $9x^4y^5$ are like terms. The coefficients are different, but the same variables are raised to the same powers. When adding polynomials, only terms that are like can be added. When adding two like terms, just add the coefficients and leave the variables alone. This process uses the distributive property. For example, $x^4y^5 + 9x^4y^5 = (1+9)x^4y^5 = 10x^4y^5$. Therefore, when adding two polynomials, simply add the like terms together. Unlike terms cannot be combined.

Subtracting polynomials involves adding the opposite of the polynomial being subtracted. Basically, the sign of each term in the polynomial being subtracted is changed, and then the like terms are combined because it is now an addition problem. For example, consider the following:

$$6x^2 - 4x + 2 - (4x^2 - 8x + 1).$$

Add the opposite of the second polynomial to obtain $6x^2 - 4x + 2 + (-4x^2 + 8x - 1)$. Then, collect like terms to obtain $2x^2 + 4x + 1$.

Multiplying and Dividing Monomials and Polynomials

Multiplying polynomials involves using the product rule for exponents that $b^m b^n = b^{m+n}$. Basically, when multiplying expressions with the same base, just add the exponents. Multiplying a monomial times a monomial involves multiplying the coefficients together and then multiplying the variables together using the product rule for exponents. For example, $8x^2y \times 4x^4y^2 = 32x^6y^3$. When multiplying a monomial times a polynomial that is not a monomial, use the distributive property to multiply each term of the polynomial times the monomial. For example, $3x(x^2 + 3x - 4) = 3x^3 + 9x^2 - 12x$. Finally, multiplying two polynomials when neither one is a monomial involves multiplying each term of the first polynomial times each term of the second polynomial. There are some shortcuts, given certain scenarios. For example, a binomial times a binomial can be found by using the *FOIL (Firsts, Outers, Inners, Lasts)* method shown here.

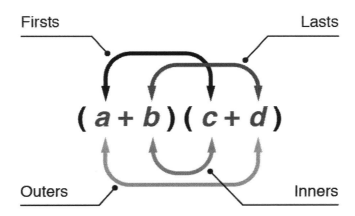

Finding the product of a sum and difference of the same two terms is simple because if it was to be foiled out, the outer and inner terms would cancel out. For instance, $(x + y)(x - y) = x^2 + xy - xy - y^2$. Finally, the square of a binomial can be found using the following formula: $(a \pm b)^2 = a^2 \pm 2ab + b^2$.

Understanding the Relationship Between Zeros and Factors of Polynomials
A *polynomial* is a mathematical expression containing the sum and difference of one or more terms that are constants multiplied times variables raised to positive powers. A *polynomial equation* is a polynomial set equal to another polynomial, or in standard form, a polynomial is set equal to 0. A *polynomial function* is a polynomial set equal to *y*. For instance, $x^2 + 2x - 8$ is a polynomial, $x^2 + 2x - 8 = 0$ is a polynomial equation, and $y = x^2 + 2x - 8$ is the corresponding polynomial function. To solve a polynomial equation, the *x*-values in which the graph of the corresponding polynomial function crosses the *x*-axis are sought. These coordinates are known as the *zeros* of the polynomial function because they are the coordinates in which the *y*-coordinates are 0. One way to find the zeros of a polynomial is to find its factors, then set each individual factor equal to 0, and solve each equation to find the zeros. A *factor* is a linear expression, and to completely factor a polynomial, the polynomial must be rewritten as a product of individual linear factors. The polynomial listed above can be factored as $(x + 4)(x - 2)$. Setting each factor equal to zero results in the zeros $x = -4$ and $x = 2$.

Here is the graph of the zeros of the polynomial:

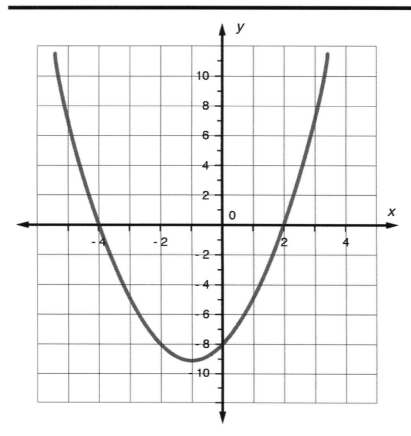

Evaluating Positive Rational Roots and Exponents

A *rational number* is any number that can be written as a fraction of two integers. Examples of rational numbers include $\frac{1}{2}, \frac{5}{4}$, and 8. The number 8 is rational because it can be expressed as a fraction also, $\frac{8}{1} = 8$. *Rational exponents* represent one way to show how roots are used to express multiplication of any number by itself. For example, 3^2 has a base of 3 and rational exponent of 2, or $\frac{2}{1}$. It can be rewritten as the square root of 3 raised to the first power, or $\sqrt[2]{3^1}$. Any number with a rational exponent can be written this way. The *numerator*, or number on top of the fraction, becomes the root and the *denominator*, or bottom number of the fraction, becomes the whole number exponent. Another example is $4^{\frac{3}{2}}$. It can be rewritten as the square root of four to the third power, or $\sqrt[2]{4^3}$. This can be simplified by performing the operations 4 to the third power, $4^3 = 4 \times 4 \times 4 = 64$, and then taking the square root of 64, $\sqrt[2]{64}$, which yields an answer of 8. Another way of stating the answer would be 4 to power $\frac{3}{2}$ is eight, or 4 times itself $\frac{3}{2}$ times is eight.

When performing operations with exponents, one must make sure that the *order of operations* is followed. Therefore, once all operations within any parentheses or grouping symbols are performed, all exponents must be evaluated before any other operation is completed. For example, to evaluate $(3-5)^2 + 4 - 5^3$, the subtraction in parentheses is done first. Then the exponents are evaluated to obtain $(-2)^2 + 4 - 5^3$, or $4 + 4 - 125$, which is equivalent to -117. A common mistake involves negative signs combined with exponents. Note that -4^2 is not equal to $(-4)^2$. The negative sign is in front of the first exponential expression, so the result is $-(4 \times 4) = -16$. However, the negative sign is inside the parentheses in the second expression, so the result is $(-4 \times -4) = 16$.

Laws of exponents can also help when performing operations with exponents. If two exponential expressions have the same base and are being multiplied, just add the exponents. For example, $2^5 \times 2^7 = 2^{5+7} = 2^{12}$. If two exponential expressions have the same base and are being divided, subtract the exponents. For example, $\frac{4^{30}}{4^2} = 4^{30-2} = 4^{28}$. If an exponential expression is being raised to another exponent, multiply the exponents together. For example, $(3^2)^5 = 3^{2\times5} = 3^{10}$.

Simplifying Algebraic Fractions

A *radical equation* is an equation that contains a variable in the *radicand*, which is the expression under the root. The radical can be a square root, a cube root, or a higher root. To solve an equation containing a root, arrange the terms so that one radical is by itself on one side of the equals sign. Then raise both sides of the equation to the value of the root. For example, square both sides if the root contains a square root, and cube both sides if the root contains a cube root. Then, solve the resulting equation. If the equation still contains a radical, those steps must be completed again to remove the equation of all radicals. Finally, it is crucial that all solutions are checked in the original equation. Some solutions to this equation, once the radicals are removed, might not be solutions to the original radical equation. Consider the following radical equation:

$$\sqrt{3x+1} - \sqrt{x+4} = 1$$

Add the second radical to both sides, and then square both sides to obtain:

$$3x + 1 = x + 4 + 2\sqrt{x+4} + 1.$$

Next, collect like terms and isolate the radical to obtain:

$$4x^2 - 16x + 16 = 4(x+4).$$

This simplifies into the quadratic equation $4x^2 - 20x$, which can be solved using factoring:

$$4x(x-5) = 0.$$

So, it has solutions, $x = 0$ and $x = 5$. Both values must be checked into the original radical equation. because $x = 0$ does not check, it is not a real solution and is called an *extraneous solution*. However, $x = 5$ is a solution.

If an equation contains a variable in the denominator of a fraction, it is known as a *rational equation*. Anything that when plugged into the equation contains a zero denominator cannot be a solution of the equation. To solve a rational equation, multiply both sides of the equation by the LCD (least common denominator) of all of the terms in the equation. Then, solve the resulting equation, making sure that the solutions do not cause any term to have a zero denominator in the original equation. Here is an example of solving the rational equation $\frac{5}{x} - \frac{1}{3} = \frac{1}{x}$:

$$3x \times \left(\frac{5}{x} - \frac{1}{3}\right) = 3x \times \left(\frac{1}{x}\right) \quad \text{Multiply both sides by the LCD}$$

$$3x \times \frac{5}{x} - 3x \times \frac{1}{3} = 3x \times \frac{1}{x} \quad \text{Distribute}$$

$$15 - x = 3 \quad \text{Simplify, and then solve}$$

$$-x = -12$$

$$x = 12$$

Both sides of the equation were initially multiplied times the LCD, $3x$. Note that the only number that could cause a problem as a solution would be $x = 0$, because it would create a 0 in the denominator.

Rewriting Simple Rational Expressions

A *rational expression* is a fraction or a ratio in which both the numerator and denominator are polynomials that are not equal to zero. A *polynomial* is a mathematical expression containing the sum and difference of one or more terms that are constants multiplied times variables raised to positive powers. Here are some examples of rational expressions: $\frac{2x^2+6x}{x}$, $\frac{x-2}{x^2-6x+8}$ and $\frac{x+2}{x^3-1}$. Such expressions can be simplified using different forms of division. The first example can be simplified in two ways. First, because the denominator is a monomial, the expression can be split up into two expressions: $\frac{2x^2}{x} + \frac{6x}{x}$, and then simplified using properties of exponents as $2x + 6$. It also can be simplified using factoring and then crossing common factors out of the numerator and denominator. For instance, it can be written as $\frac{2x(x+3)}{x} = 2(x + 3) = 2x + 6$. The second expression above can also be simplified using factoring. It can be written as $\frac{x-2}{(x-2)(x-4)} = \frac{1}{x-4}$. Finally, the third example can only be simplified using long division, as there are no common factors in the numerator and denominator. First, divide the first term of the denominator by the first term of the numerator, then write that in the quotient. Then, multiply the divisor times that number and write it below the dividend. Subtract, bring down the next term from the dividend, and continue that process with the next first term and first term of the divisor. Continue the process until every term in the divisor is accounted for.

Here is the actual long division:

Simplifying Expressions Using Long Division

$$
\begin{array}{r}
x^2 \quad\; - 2x \quad + 4 \\
x + 2 \;\big)\; x^3 \qquad\qquad\qquad\; - 1 \\
\underline{x^3 \;\; + 2x^2} \\
- 2x^2 \qquad\qquad - 1 \\
\underline{- 2x^2 \;\; - 4x} \\
4x \quad\; - 1 \\
\underline{4x \;\; + 8} \\
- 9
\end{array}
$$

Factoring

Factorization is the process of breaking up a mathematical quantity, such as a number or polynomial, into a product of two or more factors. For example, a factorization of the number 16 is $16 = 8 \times 2$. If multiplied out, the factorization results in the original number. A *prime factorization* is a specific factorization when the number is factored completely using prime numbers only. For example, the prime factorization of 16 is $16 = 2 \times 2 \times 2 \times 2$. A factor tree can be used to find the prime factorization of any number. Within a factor tree, pairs of factors are found until no other factors can be used, as in the following factor tree of the number 72:

A factor tree

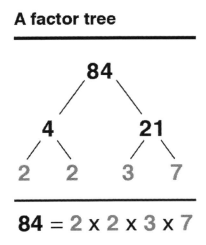

$$84 = 2 \times 2 \times 3 \times 7$$

99

It first breaks 84 into 21×4, which is not a prime factorization. Then, both 21 and 4 are factored into their primes. The final numbers on each branch consist of the numbers within the prime factorization. Therefore, $84 = 2 \times 2 \times 3 \times 7$. Factorization can be helpful in finding greatest common divisors and least common denominators.

Also, a factorization of an algebraic expression can be found. Throughout the process, a more complicated expression can be decomposed into products of simpler expressions. To factor a polynomial, first determine if there is a greatest common factor. If there is, factor it out. For example, $2x^2 + 8x$ has a greatest common factor of $2x$ and can be written as $2x(x + 4)$. Once the greatest common monomial factor is factored out, if applicable, count the number of terms in the polynomial. If there are two terms, is it a difference of squares, a sum of cubes, or a difference of cubes?

If so, the following rules can be used:

$$a^2 - b^2 = (a + b)(a - b)$$

$$a^3 + b^3 = (a + b)(a^2 - ab + b^2)$$

$$a^3 - b^3 = (a + b)(a^2 + ab + b^2)$$

If there are three terms, and if the trinomial is a perfect square trinomial, it can be factored into the following:

$$a^2 + 2ab + b^2 = (a + b)^2$$

$$a^2 - 2ab + b^2 = (a - b)^2$$

If not, try factoring into a product of two binomials by trial and error into a form of $(x + p)(x + q)$. For example, to factor $x^2 + 6x + 8$, determine what two numbers have a product of 8 and a sum of 6. Those numbers are 4 and 2, so the trinomial factors into $(x + 2)(x + 4)$.

Finally, if there are four terms, try factoring by grouping. First, group terms together that have a common monomial factor. Then, factor out the common monomial factor from the first two terms. Next, look to see if a common factor can be factored out of the second set of two terms that results in a common binomial factor. Finally, factor out the common binomial factor of each expression, for example:

$$xy - x + 5y - 5 = x(y - 1) + 5(y - 1) = (y - 1)(x + 5)$$

After the expression is completely factored, check to see if the factorization is correct by multiplying to try to obtain the original expression. Factorizations are helpful in solving equations that consist of a polynomial set equal to 0. If the product of two algebraic expressions equals 0, then at least one of the factors is equal to 0. Therefore, factor the polynomial within the equation, set each factor equal to 0, and solve. For example, $x^2 + 7x - 18 = 0$ can be solved by factoring into $(x + 9)(x - 2) = 0$. Set each factor equal to 0, and solve to obtain $x = -9$ and $x = 2$.

There are a number of ways to solve a quadratic equation. The first way is through *factoring*. If the equation is in standard form and the polynomial can be factored, set each factor equal to 0 and solve. This can be done because if $ab = 0$, either $a = 0, b = 0$, or both are equal to 0. For example, $x^2 - 7x + 10 = (x - 5)(x - 2)$. Therefore, the solutions of $x^2 - 7x + 10 = 0$ are those that satisfy both $x - 5 = 0$ and $x - 2 = 0$, or $x = 5$ and 2. This is the simplest method to solve quadratic equations; however, not all quadratic polynomials can be factored, so this method does not work for all quadratic equations.

Solution of Equations, Inequalities, and Word Problems

Solving Linear Equations and Inequalities

Solving Linear Equations
An *equation in one variable* is a mathematical statement where two algebraic expressions in one variable, usually x, are set equal. To solve the equation, the variable must be isolated on one side of the equals sign. The addition and multiplication principles of equality are used to isolate the variable. The *addition principle of equality* states that the same number can be added to or subtracted from both sides of an equation. Because the same value is being used on both sides of the equals sign, equality is maintained. For example, the equation $2x = 5x$ is equivalent to both $2x + 3 = 5x + 3$, and $2x - 5 = 5x - 5$. This principle can be used to solve the following equation: $x + 5 = 4$. The variable x must be isolated, so to move the 5 from the left side, subtract 5 from both sides of the equals sign. Therefore, $x + 5 - 5 = 4 - 5$. So, the solution is $x = -1$. This process illustrates the idea of an *additive inverse* because subtracting 5 is the same as adding -5. Basically, add the opposite of the number that must be removed to both sides of the equals sign. The *multiplication principle of equality* states that equality is maintained when a number is either multiplied times both expressions on each side of the equals sign, or when both expressions are divided by the same number. For example, $4x = 5$ is equivalent to both $16x = 20$ and $x = \frac{5}{4}$. Multiplying both sides times 4 and dividing both sides by 4 maintains equality. Solving the equation $6x - 18 = 5$ requires the use of both principles. First, apply the addition principle to add 18 to both sides of the equals sign, which results in $6x = 23$. Then use the multiplication principle to divide both sides by 6, giving the solution $x = \frac{23}{6}$. Using the multiplication principle in the solving process is the same as involving a multiplicative inverse. A *multiplicative inverse* is a value that, when multiplied by a given number, results in 1. Dividing by 6 is the same as multiplying by $\frac{1}{6}$, which is both the reciprocal and multiplicative inverse of 6.

When solving a linear equation in one variable, checking the answer shows if the solution process was performed correctly. Plug the solution into the variable in the original equation. If the result is a false statement, something was done incorrectly during the solution procedure. Checking the example above gives the following: $6 \times \frac{23}{6} - 18 = 23 - 18 = 5$. Therefore, the solution is correct.

Some equations in one variable involve fractions or the use of the distributive property. In either case, the goal is to obtain only one variable term and then use the addition and multiplication principles to isolate that variable. Consider the equation $\frac{2}{3}x = 6$. To solve for x, multiply each side of the equation by the reciprocal of $\frac{2}{3}$, which is $\frac{3}{2}$. This step results in $\frac{3}{2} \times \frac{2}{3}x = \frac{3}{2} \times 6$, which simplifies into the solution $x = 9$. Now consider the equation $3(x + 2) - 5x = 4x + 1$. Use the distributive property to clear the parentheses. Therefore, multiply each term inside the parentheses by 3. This step results in $3x + 6 - 5x = 4x + 1$. Next, collect like terms on the left-hand side. *Like terms* are terms with the same variable or variables raised to the same exponent(s). Only like terms can be combined through addition or subtraction. After collecting like terms, the equation is $-2x + 6 = 4x + 1$. Finally, apply the addition and multiplication principles. Add $2x$ to both sides to obtain $6 = 6x + 1$. Then, subtract 1 from both sides to obtain $5 = 6x$. Finally, divide both sides by 6 to obtain the solution $\frac{5}{6} = x$.

Two other types of solutions can be obtained when solving an equation in one variable. The final result could be that there is either no solution or that the solution set contains all real numbers. Consider the equation $4x = 6x + 5 - 2x$. First, the like terms can be combined on the right to obtain $4x = 4x + 5$. Next, subtract $4x$ from both sides. This step results in the false statement $0 = 5$. There is no value that can be

101

plugged into x that will ever make this equation true. Therefore, there is no solution. The solution procedure contained correct steps, but the result of a false statement means that no value satisfies the equation. The symbolic way to denote that no solution exists is $\emptyset$. Next, consider the equation $5x + 4 + 2x = 9 + 7x - 5$. Combining the like terms on both sides results in $7x + 4 = 7x + 4$. The left-hand side is exactly the same as the right-hand side. Using the addition principle to move terms, the result is $0 = 0$, which is always true. Therefore, the original equation is true for any number, and the solution set is all real numbers. The symbolic way to denote such a solution set is $\mathbb{R}$, or in interval notation, $(-\infty, \infty)$.

One-step problems take only one mathematical step to solve. For example, solving the equation $5x = 45$ is a one-step problem because the one step of dividing both sides of the equation by 5 is the only step necessary to obtain the solution $x = 9$. The multiplication principle of equality is the one step used to isolate the variable. The equation is of the form $ax = b$, where a and b are rational numbers. Similarly, the addition principle of equality could be the one step needed to solve a problem. In this case, the equation would be of the form $x + a = b$ or $x - a = b$, for real numbers a and b.

A multi-step problem involves more than one step to find the solution, or it could consist of solving more than one equation. An equation that involves both the addition principle and the multiplication principle is a two-step problem, and an example of such an equation is $2x - 4 = 5$. Solving involves adding 4 to both sides and then dividing both sides by 2. An example of a two-step problem involving two separate equations is $y = 3x, 2x + y = 4$. The two equations form a system of two equations that must be solved together in two variables. The system can be solved by the substitution method. Since y is already solved for in terms of x, plug $3x$ in for y into the equation $2x + y = 4$, resulting in $2x + 3x = 4$. Therefore, $5x = 4$ and $x = \frac{4}{5}$. Because there are two variables, the solution consists of both a value for x and for y. Substitute $x = \frac{4}{5}$ into either original equation to find y. The easiest choice is $y = 3x$. Therefore, $y = 3 \times \frac{4}{5} = \frac{12}{5}$. The solution can be written as the ordered pair $\left(\frac{4}{5}, \frac{12}{5}\right)$.

Real-world problems can be translated into both one-step and multi-step problems. In either case, the word problem must be translated from the verbal form into mathematical expressions and equations that can be solved using algebra. An example of a one-step real-world problem is the following: A cat weighs half as much as a dog living in the same house. If the dog weighs 14.5 pounds, how much does the cat weigh? To solve this problem, an equation can be used. In any word problem, the first step must be defining variables that represent the unknown quantities. For this problem, let x be equal to the unknown weight of the cat. Because two times the weight of the cat equals 14.5 pounds, the equation to be solved is: $2x = 14.5$. Use the multiplication principle to divide both sides by 2. Therefore, $x = 7.25$. The cat weighs 7.25 pounds.

Most of the time, real-world problems are more difficult than this one and consist of multi-step problems. The following is an example of a multi-step problem: The sum of two consecutive page numbers is equal to 437. What are those page numbers? First, define the unknown quantities. If x is equal to the first page number, then $x + 1$ is equal to the next page number because they are consecutive integers. Their sum is equal to 437, and this statement translates to the equation $x + x + 1 = 437$. To solve, first collect like terms to obtain $2x + 1 = 437$. Then, subtract 1 from both sides and then divide by 2. The solution to the equation is $x = 218$. Therefore, the two consecutive page numbers that satisfy the problem are 218 and 219. It is always important to make sure that answers to real-world problems make sense. For instance, if the solution to this same problem resulted in decimals, that should be a red flag indicating the need to check the work. Page numbers are whole numbers; therefore, if decimals are found to be answers, the solution process should be double-checked to see where mistakes were made.

Solving Inequalities

Inequalities can be solved in a similar method as equations. Basically, the goal is to isolate the variable, and this process can be completed by adding numbers onto both sides, subtracting numbers off of both sides, multiplying numbers onto both sides, and dividing numbers off of both sides of the inequality. Basically, if something is done to one side, it has to be done to the other side, just like when solving equations. However, there is one important difference, and that difference occurs when multiplying times negative numbers and dividing by negative numbers. If either one of these steps must be performed in the solution process, the inequality symbol must be reversed. Consider the following inequality: $2 - 3x < 11$. The goal is to isolate the variable x, so first subtract 2 off both sides to obtain $-3x < 9$. Then divide both sides by -3, making sure to "*flip the sign*." This results in $x > -3$, which is the solution set. This solution set means that all numbers greater than -3 satisfy the original inequality, and therefore any number larger than -3 is a solution. In *set-builder notation*, this set can be written as $\{x|x > -3\}$, which is read "all x values such that x is greater than -3." In addition to the inequality form of the solution, solutions of inequalities can be expressed by using both a number line and interval notation. Here is a chart that highlights all three types of expressing the solutions:

Interval Notation	Number Line Sketch	Set-builder Notation
(a , b)	a ○——————○ b	$\{x \mid a < x < b\}$
(a , b]	a ○——————● b	$\{x \mid a < x \leq b\}$
[a , b)	a ●——————○ b	$\{x \mid a \leq x < b\}$
[a , b]	a ●——————● b	$\{x \mid a \leq x \leq b\}$
(a , ∞)	a ○——————→	$\{x \mid x > a\}$
(- ∞ , b)	←——————○ b	$\{x \mid x < b\}$
[a , ∞)	a ●——————→	$\{x \mid x \geq a\}$
(- ∞ , b]	←——————● b	$\{x \mid x \leq b\}$
(- ∞, ∞)	←——————————→	$\mathbb{R}$

Solving Quadratic Equations by Factoring

A *quadratic equation* in standard form, $ax^2 + bx + c = 0$, can have either two solutions, one solution, or two complex solutions (no real solutions). This is determined using the determinant $b^2 - 4ac$. If the determinant is positive, there are two real solutions. If the determinant is negative, there are no real solutions. If the determinant is equal to 0, there is one real solution. For example, given the quadratic equation $4x^2 - 2x + 1 = 0$, its determinant is $(-2)^2 - 4(4)(1) = 4 - 16 = -12$, so it has two complex solutions, meaning no real solutions.

There are quite a few ways to solve a quadratic equation. The first is by *factoring*. If the equation is in standard form and the polynomial can be factored, set each factor equal to 0, and solve using the Principle of Zero Products. For example, $x^2 - 4x + 3 = (x - 3)(x - 1)$.

Therefore, the solutions of $x^2 - 4x + 3 = 0$ are those that satisfy both $x - 3 = 0$ and $x - 1 = 0$, or $x = 3$ and $x = 1$. This is the simplest method to solve quadratic equations; however, not all polynomials inside the quadratic equations can be factored.

Another method is *completing the square*. The polynomial $x^2 + 10x - 9$ cannot be factored, so the next option is to complete the square in the equation $x^2 + 10x - 9 = 0$ to find its solutions. The first step is to add 9 to both sides, moving the constant over to the right side, resulting in $x^2 + 10x = 9$. Then the coefficient of x is divided by 2 and squared. This result is then added to both sides of the equation. In this example, $\left(\frac{10}{2}\right)^2 = 25$ is added to both sides of the equation to obtain $x^2 + 10x + 25 = 9 + 25 = 34$. The left-hand side can then be factored into $(x + 5)^2 = 34$. Solving for x then involves taking the square root of both sides and subtracting 5. This leads to the two solutions $x = \pm\sqrt{34} - 5$.

The third method is the *quadratic formula*. Given a quadratic equation in standard form, $ax^2 + bx + c = 0$, its solutions always can be found using the formula:

$$x = \frac{-b \pm \sqrt{b^2 - 4ac}}{2a}$$

Solving Verbal Problems Presented in an Algebraic Context, Including Geometric Reasoning and Graphing

A *linear function of the form* $f(x) = mx + b$ has two important quantities: m and b. The quantity m represents the slope of the line, and the quantity b represents the y-intercept of the line. When the function represents an actual real-life situation, or mathematical model, these two quantities are very meaningful. The slope, m, represents the rate of change, or the amount y increases or decreases given an increase in x. If m is positive, the rate of change is positive, and if m is negative, the rate of change is negative. The y-intercept, b, represents the amount of the quantity y when x is 0. In many applications, if the x-variable is never a negative quantity, the y-intercept represents the initial amount of the quantity y. Often the x-variable represents time, so it makes sense that the x-variable is never negative.

Consider the following example. These two equations represent the cost, C, of t-shirts, x, at two different printing companies:

$$C(x) = 7x$$

$$C(x) = 5x + 25$$

The first equation represents a scenario that shows the cost per t-shirt is $7. In this equation, x varies directly with y. There is no y-intercept, which means that there is no initial cost for using that printing company. The rate of change is 7, which is price per shirt. The second equation represents a scenario that has both an initial cost and a cost per t-shirt. The slope 5 shows that each shirt is $5. The y-intercept 25 shows that there is an initial cost of using that company. Therefore, it makes sense to use the first company at $7 a shirt when only purchasing a small number of t-shirts. However, any large orders would be cheaper by going with the second company because eventually that initial cost will be negligible.

Interpreting Parts of Nonlinear Expressions in Terms of Their Context
If a quantity increases or decreases at a constant rate as another quantity increases, then this idea is represented as a *linear expression*, and the graph of such a relationship is a straight line. All other relationships are nonlinear, and nonlinear expressions must be used as mathematical representations of such instances.

Common nonlinear relationships that exist between two quantities are *inverse variation equations*, which are represented by equations such as $y = \frac{k}{x}$ and $y = \frac{k}{x^2}$ with constants k, quadratic equations of the form $y = ax^2 + bx + c$, and exponential equations of the form $y = a^x$.

Inverse variation situations arise when, as one quantity increases, the other quantity decreases in proportion. For instance, as a person increases the speed of a car she is driving, the time it takes to reach the destination decreases. This is a nonlinear relationship regarding inverse variation.

Recall that quadratic equations are used to model something shaped like a parabola. For example, if a ball is thrown into the air, it travels higher and higher and eventually slows down to reach its highest point, then stops dropping at a faster and faster rate. A quadratic equation must be used to tell the position of the ball given the amount of time since the ball was thrown. This relationship is nonlinear.

Finally, an *exponential equation* is used to model something with exponential growth or decay. If something grows exponentially, such as compound interest, the amount is multiplied times a growth factor for every increase in x. If something decays exponentially, the amount is multiplied times a factor between 0 and 1 for every increase in x. When a population is declining, an exponential decay equation can be used to represent the situation.

Solving, Graphing, and Modeling Multiple Types of Expressions
Translating sentences describing relationships between variables and constants to algebraic expressions and equations involves recognizing key words that represent mathematical operations. This process is known as *modeling*. For simplicity, let x be the variable, or the unknown quantity. Statements that include the four operations addition, subtraction, multiplication, and division exist in sentences that model linear relationships. For example, words and phrases that represent addition are "sum," "more than," and "increased by." Words and phrases that represent subtraction are "minus," "decreased by," "subtracted from," "difference," "less", "fewer than," and "less than." Words and phrases that represent multiplication are "times," "product of," "twice," "double," and "triple." Finally, words and phrases that represent division are "divided by," "quotient," and "reciprocal." Most of the time, these words and phrases are combined to represent expressions that deal with one or more operation. For example, "ten subtracted from nine times a number" would be represented as $9x - 10$, and "the quotient of a number and 7 increased by 8" would be represented as $\frac{x}{7} + 8$. The word problems that typically use these expressions will have a statement of equality. For instance, the problem could say "ten subtracted from nine times a number equals 20; find that number." In this case, the algebraic expression shown previously would be set equal to 20 and then solved for x.

$$9x - 10 = 20$$

Add ten to both sides and then divide by 9 to get the solution $x = \frac{30}{9}$, which reduces to $x = \frac{10}{3}$.

Other types of expressions, besides linear expressions, can be the results of modeling. If the variable is raised to a power other than 1, the result is a *polynomial expression*. The path of an object thrown up into the air is a common example of this. The graph of an object represents an upside-down parabola, which is modeled by an equation of the type $y = -ax^2$. In this case, a represents the height of the object at its highest point before coming back down to the ground, and the negative sign shows that the parabola is upside down.

Here is the graph of a parabola:

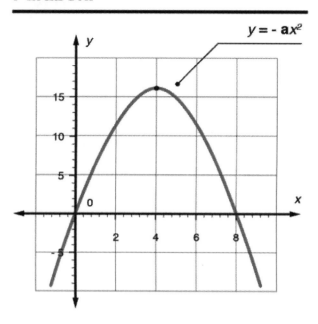

Parabola

$$y = -ax^2$$

Using Linear Relationships Represented by Graphs, Equations, and Tables, to Solve Problems
Graphs, equations, and tables are three different ways to represent linear relationships. The following graph shows a linear relationship because the relationship between the two variables is constant. As the distance increases by 25 miles, the time lapses by 1 hour. This pattern continues for the rest of the graph. The line represents a constant rate of 25 miles per hour. This graph can also be used to solve problems involving predictions for a future time. After 8 hours of travel, the rate can be used to predict the distance covered. Eight hours of travel at 25 miles per hour covers a distance of 200 miles. The equation at the top of the graph corresponds to this rate also. The same prediction of distance in a given time can be found using the equation. For a time of 10 hours, the distance would be 250 miles, as the equation yields $d = 25 \times 10 = 250$.

$$d = 25t$$

Another representation of a linear relationship can be seen in a table. The first thing to observe from the table is that the y-values increase by the same amount of 3 each time. As the x-values increase by 1, the y-values increase by 3. This pattern shows that the relationship is linear. If this table shows the money earned, y-value, for the hours worked, x-value, then it can be used to predict how much money will be earned for future hours. If 6 hours are worked, then the pay would be $19. For further hours and money to be determined, it would be helpful to have an equation that models this table of values. The equation will show the relationship between x and y. The y-value can each time be determined by multiplying the x-value by 3, then adding 1. The following equation models this relationship: $y = 3x + 1$. Now that there is an equation, any number of hours, x, can be substituted into the equation to find the amount of money earned, y.

$y = 3x + 1$	
x	y
0	1
1	4
2	7
4	13
5	16

Translating Written Phrases into Algebraic Expressions

When presented with a real-world problem that must be solved, the first step is always to determine what the unknown quantity is that must be solved for. Use a variable, such as x or t, to represent that unknown quantity. Sometimes there can be two or more unknown quantities. In this case, either choose an additional variable, or if a relationship exists between the unknown quantities, express the other quantities in terms of the original variable. After choosing the variables, form algebraic expressions and/or equations that represent the verbal statement in the problem. The following table shows examples of vocabulary used to represent the different operations.

Addition	Sum, plus, total, increase, more than, combined, in all
Subtraction	Difference, less than, subtract, reduce, decrease, fewer, remain
Multiplication	Product, multiply, times, part of, twice, triple
Division	Quotient, divide, split, each, equal parts, per, average, shared

The combination of operations and variables form both mathematical expression and equations. The difference between expressions and equations are that there is no equals sign in an expression, and that expressions are *evaluated* to find an unknown quantity, while equations are *solved* to find an unknown quantity. Also, inequalities can exist within verbal mathematical statements. Instead of a statement of equality, expressions state quantities are *less than*, *less than or equal to*, *greater than*, or *greater than or equal to*. Another type of inequality is when a quantity is said to be *not equal to* another quantity. The symbol used to represent "not equal to" is $\neq$.

The steps for solving inequalities in one variable are the same steps for solving equations in one variable. The addition and multiplication principles are used. However, to maintain a true statement when using the $<, \leq, >$, and $\geq$ symbols, if a negative number is either multiplied times both sides of an inequality or divided from both sides of an inequality, the sign must be flipped. For instance, consider the following inequality: $3 - 5x \leq 8$. First, 3 is subtracted from each side to obtain $-5x \leq 5$. Then, both sides are divided by -5, while flipping the sign, to obtain $x \geq -1$. Therefore, any real number greater than or equal to -1 satisfies the original inequality.

Practice Questions

1. What is the solution to the equation $3(x + 2) = 14x - 5$?
    a. $x = 1$
    b. No solution
    c. $x = 0$
    d. All real numbers

2. What is the solution to the equation $10 - 5x + 2 = 7x + 12 - 12x$?
    a. $x = 12$
    b. No solution
    c. $x = 0$
    d. All real numbers

3. Which of the following is the result when solving the equation $4(x + 5) + 6 = 2(2x + 3)$?
    a. Any real number is a solution.
    b. There is no solution.
    c. $x = 6$ is the solution.
    d. $x = 26$ is the solution.

4. How many cases of cola can Lexi purchase if each case is \$3.50 and she has \$40?
    a. 10
    b. 12
    c. 11.4
    d. 11

5. Two consecutive integers exist such that the sum of three times the first and two less than the second is equal to 411. What are those integers?
    a. 103 and 104
    b. 104 and 105
    c. 102 and 103
    d. 100 and 101

6. Erin and Katie work at the same ice cream shop. Together, they always work less than 21 hours a week. In a week, if Katie worked two times as many hours as Erin, how many hours could Erin work?
    a. Less than 7 hours
    b. Less than or equal to 7 hours
    c. More than 7 hours
    d. Less than 8 hours

7. Which expression is equivalent to $\sqrt[4]{x^6} - \frac{x}{x^3} + x - 2$?

    a. $x^{\frac{3}{2}} - x^2 + x - 2$

    b. $x^{\frac{2}{3}} - x^{-2} + x - 2$

    c. $x^{\frac{3}{2}} - \frac{1}{x^2} + x - 2$

    d. $x^{\frac{2}{3}} - \frac{1}{x^2} + x - 2$

8. How many possible positive zeros does the polynomial function $f(x) = x^4 - 3x^3 + 2x + x - 3$ have?

    a. 4

    b. 3

    c. 2

    d. 1

9. What is the solution to the following linear inequality?

$$7 - \frac{4}{5}x < \frac{3}{5}$$

    a. $(-\infty, 8)$

    b. $(8, \infty)$

    c. $[8, \infty)$

    d. $(-\infty, 8]$

10. Triple the difference of five and a number is equal to the sum of that number and 5. What is the number?

    a. 5

    b. 2

    c. 5.5

    d. 2.5

11. What is an equivalent form of the rational expression $\sqrt{200x^6y^7z^2}$? Assume all variables represent positive real numbers.

    a. $20x^3y^3z\sqrt{y}$

    b. $10x^3y^3z\sqrt{2y}$

    c. $10xyz\sqrt{2xyz}$

    d. $10x^2y^3z\sqrt{2z}$

12. What is the simplified form of $(4y^3)^4(3y^7)^2$?

    a. $12y^{26}$

    b. $2304y^{16}$

    c. $12y^{14}$

    d. $2304y^{26}$

Answer Explanations

1. A: First, the distributive property must be used on the left side. This results in $3x + 6 = 14x - 5$. The addition property is then used to add 5 to both sides, and then to subtract $3x$ from both sides, resulting in $11 = 11x$. Finally, the multiplication property is used to divide each side by 11. Therefore, $x = 1$ is the solution.

2. D: First, like terms are collected to obtain $12 - 5x = -5x + 12$. Then, if the addition principle is used to move the terms with the variable, $5x$ is added to both sides, and the mathematical statement $12 = 12$ is obtained. This is always true; therefore, all real numbers satisfy the original equation.

3. B: The distributive property is used on both sides to obtain $4x + 20 + 6 = 4x + 6$. Then, like terms are collected on the left, resulting in $4x + 26 = 4x + 6$. Next, the addition principle is used to subtract $4x$ from both sides, and this results in the false statement $26 = 6$. Therefore, there is no solution.

4. D: This is a one-step real-world application problem. The unknown quantity is the number of cases of cola to be purchased. Let x be equal to this amount. Because each case costs $3.50, the total number of cases times $3.50 must equal $40. This translates to the mathematical equation $3.5x = 40$. Divide both sides by 3.5 to obtain $x = 11.4286$, which has been rounded to four decimal places. Because cases are sold whole (the store does not sell portions of cases), and there is not enough money to purchase 12 cases, there is only enough money to purchase 11.

5. A: First, the variables have to be defined. Let x be the first integer; therefore, $x + 1$ is the second integer. This is a two-step problem. The sum of three times the first and two less than the second is translated into the following expression: $3x + (x + 1 - 2)$. This expression is set equal to 411 to obtain $3x + (x + 1 - 2) = 411$. The left-hand side is simplified to obtain $4x - 1 = 411$. The addition and multiplication properties are used to solve for x. First, add 1 to both sides and then divide both sides by 4 to obtain $x = 103$. The next consecutive integer is 104.

6. A: Let x be the unknown, the number of hours Erin can work. We know Katie works $2x$, and the sum of all hours is less than 21. Therefore, $x + 2x < 21$, which simplifies into $3x < 21$. Solving this results in the inequality $x < 7$ after dividing both sides by 3. Therefore, Erin can work less than 7 hours.

7. C: By switching from a radical expression to rational exponents, $\sqrt[4]{x^6} = x^{\frac{6}{4}} = x^{\frac{3}{2}}$. Also, properties of exponents can be used to simplify $\frac{x}{x^3}$ into $x^{1-3} = x^{-2} = \frac{1}{x^2}$. The other terms can be left alone, resulting in an equivalent expression $x^{\frac{3}{2}} - \frac{1}{x^2} + x - 2$.

8. B: Using Descartes' Rule of Signs, count the number of sign changes in coefficients in the polynomial. This results in the number of possible positive zeros. The coefficients are 1, -3, 2, 1, and -3, so the sign changes from 1 to -3, -3 to 2, and 1 to -3, a total of 3 times. Therefore, there are at most 3 positive zeros.

9. B: The goal is to first isolate the variable. The fractions can easily be cleared by multiplying the entire inequality by 5, resulting in $35 - 4x < 3$. Then, subtract 35 from both sides and divide by -4. This results in $x > 8$. Notice the inequality symbol has been flipped because both sides were divided by a negative number. The solution set, all real numbers greater than 8, is written in interval notation as $(8, \infty)$. A parenthesis shows that 8 is not included in the solution set.

10. D: Let x be the missing quantity. The problem can be expressed as the following equation: $3(5 - x) = x + 5$. Distributing the 3 results in $15 - 3x = x + 5$. Subtract 5 from both sides, add $3x$ to both sides, and then divide both sides by 4. This results in $\frac{10}{4} = \frac{5}{2} = 2.5$.

11. B: The expression under the radical can be factored into perfect squares as such: $\sqrt{100 \times 2 \times x^6 \times y^6 \times y \times z^2}$. Using rational exponents, this is the same as

$$(100 \times 2 \times x^6 \times y^6 \times y \times z^2)^{\frac{1}{2}}$$

$$100^{\frac{1}{2}} \times 2^{\frac{1}{2}} \times x^{\frac{6}{2}} \times y^{\frac{6}{2}} \times y^{\frac{1}{2}} \times z^{\frac{2}{2}}$$

$$\sqrt{100} \times \sqrt{2} \times x^3 \times \sqrt{y} \times z$$

$$10x^3y^3z\sqrt{2y}$$

12. D: The exponential rules $(ab)^m = a^m b^m$ and $(a^m)^n = a^{mn}$ can be used to rewrite the expression as $4^4 y^{12} \times 3^2 y^{14}$. The coefficients are multiplied together and the exponential rule $a^m a^n = a^{m+n}$ is then used to obtain the simplified form $2304y^{26}$.

Reading Comprehension

Summarizing a Complex Text

An important skill is the ability to read a complex text and then reduce its length and complexity by focusing on the key events and details. A summary is a shortened version of the original text, written by the reader in their own words. The summary should be shorter than the original text, and it must be thoughtfully formed to include critical points from the original text.

In order to effectively summarize a complex text, it's necessary to understand the original source and identify the major points covered. It may be helpful to outline the original text to get the big picture and avoid getting bogged down in the minor details. For example, a summary wouldn't include a statistic from the original source unless it was the major focus of the text. It's also important for readers to use their own words yet retain the original meaning of the passage. The key to a good summary is emphasizing the main idea without changing the focus of the original information.

The more complex a text, the more difficult it can be to summarize. Readers must evaluate all points from the original source and then filter out what they feel are the less necessary details. Only the essential ideas should remain. The summary often mirrors the original text's organizational structure. For example, in a problem-solution text structure, the author typically presents readers with a problem and then develops solutions through the course of the text. An effective summary would likely retain this general structure, rephrasing the problem and then reporting the most useful or plausible solutions.

Paraphrasing is somewhat similar to summarizing. It calls for the reader to take a small part of the passage and list or describe its main points. Paraphrasing is more than rewording the original passage, though. Like summary, it should be written in the reader's own words, while still retaining the meaning of the original source. The main difference between summarizing and paraphrasing is that a summary would be appropriate for a much larger text, while paraphrase might focus on just a few lines of text. Effective paraphrasing will indicate an understanding of the original source, yet still help the reader expand on their interpretation. A paraphrase should neither add new information nor remove essential facts that change the meaning of the source.

Topic, Main Idea, and Supporting Details

The *topic* of a text is the general subject matter. Text topics can usually be expressed in one word, or a few words at most. Additionally, readers should ask themselves what point the author is trying to make. This point is the *main idea* or *primary purpose* of the text, the one thing the author wants readers to know concerning the topic. Once the author has established the main idea, they will support the main idea by supporting details. Supporting details are evidence that support the main idea and include personal testimonies, examples, or statistics.

One analogy for these components and their relationships is that a text is like a well-designed house. The topic is the roof, covering all rooms. The main idea is the frame. The supporting details are the various rooms. To identify the topic of a text, readers can ask themselves what or who the author is writing about in the paragraph. To locate the main idea, readers can ask themselves what one idea the author wants readers to know about the topic. To identify supporting details, readers can put the main idea into question form and ask, "what does the author use to prove or explain their main idea?"

Let's look at an example. An author is writing an essay about the Amazon rainforest and trying to convince the audience that more funding should go into protecting the area from deforestation. The author makes the argument stronger by including evidence of the benefits of the rainforest: it provides habitats to a variety of species, it provides much of the earth's oxygen which in turn cleans the atmosphere, and it is the home to medicinal plants that may be the answer to some of the world's deadliest diseases. Here is an outline of the essay looking at topic, main idea, and supporting details:

- Topic: Amazon rainforest
- Main Idea: The Amazon rainforest should receive more funding in order to protect it from deforestation.
- Supporting Details:
    - 1. It provides habitats to a variety of species
    - 2. It provides much of the earth's oxygen which in turn cleans the atmosphere
    - 3. It is home to medicinal plants that may be the answer to some of the world's deadliest diseases.

Notice that the topic of the essay is listed in a few key words: "Amazon rainforest." The main idea tells us what about the topic is important: that the topic should be funded in order to prevent deforestation. Finally, the supporting details are what the author relies on to convince the audience to act or to believe in the truth of the main idea.

Information that is Explicitly Stated

In the Reading Comprehension section, test takers will be asked questions based on their direct knowledge of the passage. The information explicitly stated in the passage leaves the reader no room for confusion. The sections below allow test takers to determine what type of information is explicitly stated in the passage. Is the information an author's opinion or an objective fact? Does the information contain bias or stereotype? And within the information stated, what words are directly stated and what words leave room for a connotative interpretation? Being cautious of the author's presentation of information will aid the test taker in determining the correct answer choice for the question stem.

Facts and Opinions
A fact is a statement that is true empirically or an event that has actually occurred in reality and can be proven or supported by evidence; it is generally objective. In contrast, an opinion is subjective, representing something that someone believes rather than something that exists in the absolute. People's individual understandings, feelings, and perspectives contribute to variations in opinion. Though facts are typically objective in nature, in some instances, a statement of fact may be both factual and yet also subjective. For example, emotions are individual subjective experiences. If an individual says that they feel happy or sad, the feeling is subjective, but the statement is factual; hence, it is a subjective fact. In contrast, if one person tells another that the other is feeling happy or sad—whether this is true or not—that is an assumption or an opinion.

Biases
Biases usually occur when someone allows their personal preferences or ideologies to interfere with what should be an objective decision. In personal situations, someone is biased towards someone if they favor them in an unfair way. In academic writing, being biased in your sources means leaving out objective information that would turn the argument one way or the other. The evidence of bias in academic writing makes the text less credible, so be sure to present all viewpoints when writing, not just your own, so to avoid coming off as biased. Being objective when presenting information or dealing with people usually allows the author to gain more credibility.

Stereotypes

Stereotypes are preconceived notions that place a particular rule or characteristics on an entire group of people. Stereotypes are usually offensive to the group they refer to or allies of that group, and often have negative connotations. The reinforcement of stereotypes isn't always obvious. Sometimes stereotypes can be very subtle and are still widely used in order for people to understand categories within the world. For example, saying that women are more intuitive or nurturing than men is a stereotype, although this is still an assumption used by many in order to understand differences between one another.

Denotation and Connotation

Denotation refers to a word's explicit definition, like that found in the dictionary. Denotation is often set in comparison to connotation. Connotation is the emotional, cultural, social, or personal implication associated with a word. Denotation is more of an objective definition, whereas connotation can be more subjective, although many connotative meanings of words are similar for certain cultures. The denotative meanings of words are usually based on facts, and the connotative meanings of words are usually based on emotion. Here are some examples of words and their denotative and connotative meanings in Western culture:

Word	Denotative Meaning	Connotative Meaning
Home	A permanent place where one lives, usually as a member of a family.	A place of warmth; a place of familiarity; comforting; a place of safety and security. "Home" usually has a positive connotation.
Snake	A long reptile with no limbs and strong jaws that moves along the ground; some snakes have a poisonous bite.	An evil omen; a slithery creature (human or nonhuman) that is deceitful or unwelcome. "Snake" usually has a negative connotation.
Winter	A season of the year that is the coldest, usually from December to February in the northern hemisphere and from June to August in the southern hemisphere.	Circle of life, especially that of death and dying; cold or icy; dark and gloomy; hibernation, sleep, or rest. Winter can have a negative connotation, although many who have access to heat may enjoy the snowy season from their homes.

Information or Ideas that can be Inferred

One technique authors often use to make their fictional stories more interesting is not giving away too much information by providing hints and descriptions. It is then up to the reader to draw a conclusion about the author's meaning by connecting textual clues with the reader's own pre-existing experiences and knowledge. Drawing conclusions is important as a reading strategy for understanding what is occurring in a text. Rather than directly stating who, what, where, when, or why, authors often describe story elements. Then, readers must draw conclusions to understand significant story components. As they go through a text, readers can think about the setting, characters, plot, problem, and solution; whether the author provided any clues for consideration; and combine any story clues with their existing knowledge and experiences to draw conclusions about what occurs in the text.

Making Predictions

Before and during reading, readers can apply the strategy of making predictions about what they think may happen next. For example, what plot and character developments will occur in fiction? What points will the author discuss in nonfiction? Making predictions about portions of text they have not yet read prepares readers mentally, and also gives them a purpose for reading. To inform and make predictions about text, the reader can do the following:

- Consider the title of the text and what it implies
- Look at the cover of the book
- Look at any illustrations or diagrams for additional visual information
- Analyze the structure of the text
- Apply outside experience and knowledge to the text

Readers may adjust their predictions as they read. Reader predictions may or may not come true in text.

Making Inferences

Authors describe settings, characters, character emotions, and events. Readers must infer to understand the text fully. Inferring enables readers to figure out meanings of unfamiliar words, make predictions about upcoming text, draw conclusions, and reflect on reading. Readers can infer about text before, during, and after reading. In everyday life, we use sensory information to infer. Readers can do the same with text. When authors do not answer all reader questions, readers must infer by looking at illustrations, considering characters' behaviors, and asking questions during reading. Taking clues from text and connecting text to prior knowledge help to draw conclusions. Readers can infer word meanings, settings, reasons for occurrences, character emotions, pronoun referents, author messages, and answers to questions unstated in text.

Making inferences and drawing conclusions involve skills that are quite similar: both require readers to fill in information the author has omitted. Authors may omit information as a technique for inducing readers to discover the outcomes themselves; or they may consider certain information unimportant; or they may assume their reading audience already knows certain information. To make an inference or draw a conclusion about text, readers should observe all facts and arguments the author has presented and consider what they already know from their own personal experiences. Reading students taking multiple-choice tests that refer to text passages can determine correct and incorrect choices based on the information in the passage. For example, from a text passage describing an individual's signs of anxiety while unloading groceries and nervously clutching their wallet at a grocery store checkout, readers can infer or conclude that the individual may not have enough money to pay for everything.

Inferring the Logical Conclusion from a Reading Selection

Making an inference from a selection means to make an educated guess from the passage read. Inferences should be conclusions based off of sound evidence and reasoning. When multiple-choice test questions ask about the logical conclusion that can be drawn from reading text, the test-taker must identify which choice will unavoidably lead to that conclusion. In order to eliminate the incorrect choices, the test-taker should come up with a hypothetical situation wherein an answer choice is true, but the conclusion is not true. For example, here is an example with three answer choices:

Fred purchased the newest PC available on the market. Therefore, he purchased the most expensive PC in the computer store.

What can one assume for this conclusion to follow logically?

a. Fred enjoys purchasing expensive items.
b. PCs are some of the most expensive personal technology products available.
c. The newest PC is the most expensive one.

The premise of the text is the first sentence: Fred purchased the newest PC. The conclusion is the second sentence: Fred purchased the most expensive PC. Recent release and price are two different factors; the difference between them is the logical gap. To eliminate the gap, one must equate whatever new information the conclusion introduces with the pertinent information the premise has stated. This example simplifies the process by having only one of each: one must equate product recency with product price. Therefore, a possible bridge to the logical gap could be a sentence stating that the newest PCs always cost the most.

The Purpose of Words or Phrases as Used in Context

Readers can often figure out what unfamiliar words mean without interrupting their reading to look them up in dictionaries by examining context. Context includes the other words or sentences in a passage. One common context clue is the root word and any affixes (prefixes/suffixes). Another common context clue is a synonym or definition included in the sentence. Sometimes both exist in the same sentence. Here's an example:

Scientists who study birds are *ornithologists*.

Many readers may not know the word *ornithologist*. However, the example contains a definition (scientists who study birds). The reader may also have the ability to analyze the suffix (-*logy*, meaning the study of) and root (*ornitho-*, meaning bird).

Another common context clue is a sentence that shows differences. Here's an example:

Birds *incubate* their eggs outside of their bodies, unlike mammals.

Some readers may be unfamiliar with the word *incubate*. However, since we know that "unlike mammals," birds incubate their eggs outside of their bodies, we can infer that *incubate* has something to do with keeping eggs warm outside the body until they are hatched.

In addition to analyzing the etymology of a word's root and affixes and extrapolating word meaning from sentences that contrast an unknown word with an antonym, readers can also determine word meanings from sentence context clues based on logic. Here's an example:

Birds are always looking out for predators that could attack their young.

The reader who is unfamiliar with the word *predator* could determine from the context of the sentence that predators usually prey upon baby birds and possibly other young animals. Readers might also use the context clue of etymology here, as *predator* and *prey* have the same root.

When readers encounter an unfamiliar word in text, they can use the surrounding context—the overall subject matter, specific chapter/section topic, and especially the immediate sentence context. Among others, one category of context clues is grammar. For example, the position of a word in a sentence and its relationship to the other words can help the reader establish whether the unfamiliar word is a verb, a noun, an adjective, an adverb, etc. This narrows down the possible meanings of the word to one part of speech. However, this may be insufficient. In a sentence that many birds *migrate* twice yearly, the reader can determine the word is a verb, and probably does not mean eat or drink; but it could mean travel, mate, lay eggs, hatch, or molt.

Some words can have a number of different meanings depending on how they are used. For example, the word *fly* has a different meaning in each of the following sentences:

- "His trousers have a fly on them."
- "He swatted the fly on his trousers."
- "Those are some fly trousers."
- "They went fly fishing."
- "She hates to fly."
- "If humans were meant to fly, they would have wings."

As strategies, readers can try substituting a familiar word for an unfamiliar one and see whether it makes sense in the sentence. They can also identify other words in a sentence, offering clues to an unfamiliar word's meaning.

The Organization or Structure

Text structure is the way in which the author organizes and presents textual information so readers can follow and comprehend it. One kind of text structure is sequence. This means the author arranges the text in a logical order from beginning to middle to end. There are three types of sequences:

- Chronological: ordering events in time from earliest to latest

- Spatial: describing objects, people, or spaces according to their relationships to one another in space

- Order of Importance: addressing topics, characters, or ideas according to how important they are, from either least important to most important

Chronological sequence is the most common sequential text structure. Readers can identify sequential structure by looking for words that signal it, like *first, earlier, meanwhile, next, then, later, finally,* and specific times and dates the author includes as chronological references.

Problem-Solution Text Structure
The problem-solution text structure organizes textual information by presenting readers with a problem and then developing its solution throughout the course of the text. The author may present a variety of alternatives as possible solutions, eliminating each as they are found unsuccessful, or gradually leading up to the ultimate solution. For example, in fiction, an author might write a murder mystery novel and have the character(s) solve it through investigating various clues or character alibis until the killer is identified. In nonfiction, an author writing an essay or book on a real-world problem might discuss various alternatives and explain their disadvantages or why they would not work before identifying the best solution. For scientific research, an author reporting and discussing scientific experiment results would explain why various alternatives failed or succeeded.

Comparison-Contrast Text Structure

Comparison identifies similarities between two or more things. *Contrast* identifies differences between two or more things. Authors typically employ both to illustrate relationships between things by highlighting their commonalities and deviations. For example, a writer might compare Windows and Linux as operating systems, and contrast Linux as free and open-source vs. Windows as proprietary. When writing an essay, sometimes it is useful to create an image of the two objects or events you are comparing or contrasting. Venn diagrams are useful because they show the differences as well as the similarities between two things. Once you've seen the similarities and differences on paper, it might be helpful to create an outline of the essay with both comparison and contrast. Every outline will look different, because every two or more things will have a different number of comparisons and contrasts. Say you are trying to compare and contrast carrots with sweet potatoes. Here is an example of a compare/contrast outline using those topics:

- Introduction: Talk about why you are comparing and contrasting carrots and sweet potatoes. Give the thesis statement.
- Body paragraph 1: Sweet potatoes and carrots are both root vegetables (similarity)
- Body paragraph 2: Sweet potatoes and carrots are both orange (similarity)
- Body paragraph 3: Sweet potatoes and carrots have different nutritional components (difference)
- Conclusion: Restate the purpose of your comparison/contrast essay.

Of course, if there is only one similarity between your topics and two differences, you will want to rearrange your outline. Always tailor your essay to what works best with your topic.

Descriptive Text Structure

Description can be both a type of text structure and a type of text. Some texts are descriptive throughout entire books. For example, a book may describe the geography of a certain country, state, or region, or tell readers all about dolphins by describing many of their characteristics. Many other texts are not descriptive throughout but use descriptive passages within the overall text. The following are a few examples of descriptive text:

- When the author describes a character in a novel
- When the author sets the scene for an event by describing the setting
- When a biographer describes the personality and behaviors of a real-life individual
- When a historian describes the details of a particular battle within a book about a specific war
- When a travel writer describes the climate, people, foods, and/or customs of a certain place

A hallmark of description is using sensory details, painting a vivid picture so readers can imagine it almost as if they were experiencing it personally.

Cause and Effect Text Structure

When using cause and effect to extrapolate meaning from text, readers must determine the cause when the author only communicates effects. For example, if a description of a child eating an ice cream cone includes details like beads of sweat forming on the child's face and the ice cream dripping down her hand faster than she can lick it off, the reader can infer or conclude it must be hot outside. A useful technique for making such decisions is wording them in "If/then" form, like the following: "If the child is perspiring and the ice cream melting, it must be a hot day." Cause and effect text structures explain why certain events or actions resulted in particular outcomes. For example, an author might describe America's historical large flocks of dodo birds, the fact that gunshots did not startle/frighten dodos, and that because dodos did not flee, settlers killed whole flocks in one hunting session, explaining how the dodo was hunted into extinction.

Recognizing Events in a Sequence

Sequence structure is the order of events in which a story or information is presented to the audience. Sometimes the text will be presented in chronological order, or sometimes it will be presented by displaying the most recent information first, then moving backwards in time. The sequence structure depends on the author, the context, and the audience. The structure of a text also depends on the genre in which the text is written. Is it literary fiction? Is it a magazine article? Is it instructions for how to complete a certain task? Different genres will have different purposes for switching up the sequence of their writing.

Narrative Structure

The structure presented in literary fiction is also known as *narrative structure*. Narrative structure is the foundation on which the text moves. The basic ways for moving the text along are in the plot and the setting. The plot is the sequence of events in the narrative that move the text forward through cause and effect. The setting of a story is the place or time period in which the story takes place. Narrative structure has two main categories: linear and nonlinear.

Linear Narrative

Linear narrative is a narrative told in chronological order. Traditional linear narratives will follow the plot diagram below depicting the narrative arc. The narrative arc consists of the exposition, conflict, rising action, climax, falling action, and resolution.

- Exposition: The exposition is in the beginning of a narrative and introduces the characters, setting, and background information of the story. The importance of the exposition lies in its framing of the upcoming narrative. Exposition literally means "a showing forth" in Latin.

- Conflict: The conflict, in a traditional narrative, is presented toward the beginning of the story after the audience becomes familiar with the characters and setting. The conflict is a single instance between characters, nature, or the self, in which the central character is forced to make a decision or move forward with some kind of action. The conflict presents something for the main character, or protagonist, to overcome.

- Rising Action: The rising action is the part of the story that leads into the climax. The rising action will feature the development of characters and plot and creates the tension and suspense that eventually lead to the climax.

- Climax: The climax is the part of the story where the tension produced in the rising action comes to a culmination. The climax is the peak of the story. In a traditional structure, everything before the climax builds up to it, and everything after the climax falls from it. It is the height of the narrative and is usually either the most exciting part of the story or is marked by some turning point in the character's journey.

- Falling Action: The falling action happens as a result of the climax. Characters continue to develop, although there is a wrapping up of loose ends here. The falling action leads to the resolution.

- Resolution: The resolution is where the story comes to an end and usually leaves the reader with the satisfaction of knowing what happened within the story and why. However, stories do not always end in this fashion. Sometimes readers can be confused or frustrated at the end from lack of information or the absence of a happy ending.

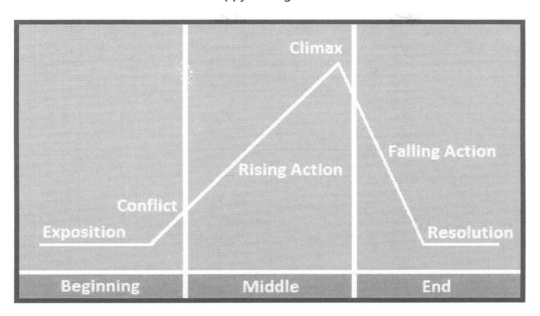

Nonlinear Narrative

A nonlinear narrative deviates from the traditional narrative in that it does not always follow the traditional plot structure of the narrative arc. Nonlinear narratives may include structures that are disjointed, circular, or disruptive, in the sense that they do not follow chronological order, but rather a nontraditional order of structure. *In medias res* is an example of a structure that predates the linear narrative. *In medias res* is Latin for "in the middle of things," which is how many ancient texts, especially epic poems, began their story, such as Homer's *Iliad.* Instead of having a clear exposition with a full development of characters, they would begin right in the middle of the action.

Modernist texts in the late nineteenth and early twentieth century are known for their experimentation with disjointed narratives, moving away from traditional linear narrative. Disjointed narratives are depicted in novels like *Catch 22*, where the author, Joseph Heller, structures the narrative based on free association of ideas rather than chronology. Another nonlinear narrative can be seen in the novel *Wuthering Heights*, written by Emily Bronte, which disrupts the chronological order by being told retrospectively after the first chapter. There seem to be two narratives in *Wuthering Heights* working at the same time: a present narrative as well as a past narrative. Authors employ disrupting narratives for various reasons; some use it for the purpose of creating situational irony for the readers, while some use it to create a certain effect in the reader, such as excitement, or even a feeling of discomfort or fear.

Sequence Structure in Technical Documents

The purpose of technical documents, such as instructions manuals, cookbooks, or "user-friendly" documents, is to provide information to users as clearly and efficiently as possible. In order to do this, the sequence structure in technical documents that should be used is one that is as straightforward as possible. This usually involves some kind of chronological order or a direct sequence of events. For example, someone who is reading an instruction manual on how to set up their Smart TV wants directions in a clear, simple, straightforward manner that does not leave the reader to guess at the proper sequence or lead to confusion.

Sequence Structure in Informational Texts

The structure in informational texts depends again on the genre. For example, a newspaper article may start by stating an exciting event that happened, and then move on to talk about that event in chronological order, known as *sequence* or *order structure*. Many informational texts also use *cause and effect structure*, which describes an event and then identifies reasons for why that event occurred. Some essays may write about their subjects by way of *comparison and contrast*, which is a structure that compares two things or contrasts them to highlight their differences. Other documents, such as proposals, will have a *problem to solution structure*, where the document highlights some kind of problem and then offers a solution toward the end. Finally, some informational texts are written with lush details and description in order to captivate the audience, allowing them to visualize the information presented to them. This type of structure is known as *descriptive*.

Identifying Primary Sources in Various Media

A primary source is a piece of original work. This can include books, musical compositions, recordings, movies, works of visual art (paintings, drawings, photographs), jewelry, pottery, clothing, furniture, and other artifacts. Within books, primary sources may be of any genre. Whether nonfiction based on actual events or a fictional creation, the primary source relates the author's firsthand view of some specific event, phenomenon, character, place, process, ideas, field of study or discipline, or other subject matter. Whereas primary sources are original treatments of their subjects, secondary sources are a step removed from the original subjects; they analyze and interpret primary sources. These include journal articles, newspaper or magazine articles, works of literary criticism, political commentaries, and academic textbooks.

In the field of history, primary sources frequently include documents that were created around the same time period that they were describing, and most often produced by someone who had direct experience or knowledge of the subject matter. In contrast, secondary sources present the ideas and viewpoints of other authors about the primary sources; in history, for example, these can include books and other written works about the particular historical periods or eras in which the primary sources were produced. Primary sources pertinent in history include diaries, letters, statistics, government information, and original journal articles and books. In literature, a primary source might be a literary novel, a poem or book of poems, or a play. Secondary sources addressing primary sources may be criticism, dissertations, theses, and journal articles. Tertiary sources, typically reference works referring to primary and secondary sources, include encyclopedias, bibliographies, handbooks, abstracts, and periodical indexes.

In scientific fields, when scientists conduct laboratory experiments to answer specific research questions and test hypotheses, lab reports and reports of research results constitute examples of primary sources. When researchers produce statistics to support or refute hypotheses, those statistics are primary sources. When a scientist is studying some subject longitudinally or conducting a case study, they may keep a journal or diary. For example, Charles Darwin kept diaries of extensive notes on his studies during sea voyages on the *Beagle*, visits to the Galápagos Islands, etc.; Jean Piaget kept journals of observational notes for case studies of children's learning behaviors. Many scientists, particularly in past centuries, shared and discussed discoveries, questions, and ideas with colleagues through letters, which also constitute primary sources. When a scientist seeks to replicate another's experiment, the reported results, analysis, and commentary on the original work is a secondary source, as is a student's dissertation if it analyzes or discusses others' work rather than reporting original research or ideas.

Practice Questions

Short Answer

Read the statement or passage and then choose the best answer to the question. Answer the question based on what is stated or implied in the statement or passage.

1. Rehabilitation rather than punitive justice is becoming much more popular in prisons around the world. Prisons in America, especially, where the recidivism rate is 67 percent, would benefit from mimicking prison tactics in Norway, which has a recidivism rate of only 20 percent. In Norway, the idea is that a rehabilitated prisoner is much less likely to offend than one harshly punished. Rehabilitation includes proper treatment for substance abuse, psychotherapy, healthcare and dental care, and education programs.

Which of the following best captures the author's purpose?
    a. To show the audience one of the effects of criminal rehabilitation by comparison.
    b. To persuade the audience to donate to American prisons for education programs.
    c. To convince the audience of the harsh conditions of American prisons.
    d. To inform the audience of the incredibly lax system of Norway prisons.

2. What a lark! What a plunge! For so it had always seemed to her, when, with a little squeak of the hinges, which she could hear now, she had burst open the French windows and plunged at Bourton into the open air. How fresh, how calm, stiller than this of course, the air was in the early morning; like the flap of a wave; the kiss of a wave; chill and sharp and yet (for a girl of eighteen as she then was) solemn, feeling as she did, standing there at the open window, that something awful was about to happen; looking at the flowers, at the trees with the smoke winding off them and the rooks rising, falling; standing and looking until Peter Walsh said, "Musing among the vegetables?"— was that it? —"I prefer men to cauliflowers"— was that it? He must have said it at breakfast one morning when she had gone out on to the terrace — Peter Walsh. He would be back from India one of these days, June or July, she forgot which, for his letters were awfully dull; it was his sayings one remembered; his eyes, his pocket-knife, his smile, his grumpiness and, when millions of things had utterly vanished — how strange it was! — a few sayings like this about cabbages.

From Mrs. Dalloway by Virginia Woolf

What was the narrator feeling right before Peter Walsh's voice distracted her?
    a. A spark of excitement for the morning.
    b. Anger at the larks.
    c. A sense of foreboding.
    d. Confusion at the weather.

3. According to the plan of the convention, all judges who may be appointed by the United States are to hold their offices *during good behavior*, which is conformable to the most approved of the State constitutions and among the rest, to that of this State. Its propriety having been drawn into question by the adversaries of that plan, is no light symptom of the rage for objection, which disorders their imaginations and judgments. The standard of good behavior for the continuance in office of the judicial magistracy, is certainly one of the most valuable of the modern improvements in the practice of government. In a monarchy it is an excellent barrier to the despotism of the prince; in a republic it is a no less excellent barrier to the encroachments and oppressions of the representative body. And it is the best

expedient which can be devised in any government, to secure a steady, upright, and impartial administration of the laws.

From *The Federalist No. 78* by Alexander Hamilton

What is Hamilton's point in this excerpt?
   a. To show the audience that despotism within a monarchy is no longer the standard practice in the states.
   b. To convince the audience that judges holding their positions based on good behavior is a practical way to avoid corruption.
   c. To persuade the audience that having good behavior should be the primary characteristic of a person in a government body and their voting habits should reflect this.
   d. To convey the position that judges who serve for a lifetime will not be perfect and therefore we must forgive them for their bad behavior when it arises.

4. There was a man named Webster lived in a town of twenty-five thousand people in the state of Wisconsin. He had a wife named Mary and a daughter named Jane and he was himself a fairly prosperous manufacturer of washing machines. When the thing happened of which I am about to write he was thirty-seven or thirty-eight years old and his one child, the daughter, was seventeen. Of the details of his life up to the time a certain revolution happened within him it will be unnecessary to speak. He was however a rather quiet man inclined to have dreams which he tried to crush out of himself in order that he function as a washing machine manufacturer; and no doubt, at odd moments, when he was on a train going some place or perhaps on Sunday afternoons in the summer when he went alone to the deserted office of the factory and sat several hours looking out at a window and along a railroad track, he gave way to dreams.

from *Many Marriages* by Sherwood Anderson

What does the author mean by the following sentence?

"Of the details of his life up to the time a certain revolution happened within him it will be unnecessary to speak."

   a. The details of his external life don't matter; only the details of his internal life matter.
   b. Whatever happened in his life before he had a certain internal change is irrelevant.
   c. He had a traumatic experience earlier in his life which rendered it impossible for him to speak.
   d. Before the revolution, he was a lighthearted man who always wished to speak to others no matter who they were.

5. The old castle soon proved to be too small for the family, and in September 1853 the foundation-stone of a new house was laid. After the ceremony the workmen were entertained at dinner, which was followed by Highland games and dancing in the ballroom.

Two years later they entered the new castle, which the Queen described as "charming; the rooms delightful; the furniture, papers, everything perfection."

The Prince was untiring in planning improvements, and in 1856 the Queen wrote: "Every year my heart becomes more fixed in this dear Paradise, and so much more so now, that *all* has become my dearest Albert's *own* creation, own work, own building, own laying out as at Osborne; and his great taste, and the impress of his dear hand, have been stamped everywhere. He was very busy today, settling and arranging many things for next year."

from the biography Queen Victoria by E. Gordon Browne, M.A.

What does the word *impress* mean in the third paragraph?
    a. To affect strongly in feeling
    b. To urge something to be done
    c. To impose a certain quality upon
    d. To press a thing onto something else

6. Having completed these preparations, Mr. Booth entered the theater by the stage door; summoned one of the scene shifters, Mr. John Spangler, emerged through the same door with that individual, leaving the door open, and left the mare in his hands to be held until he (Booth) should return. Booth who was even more fashionably and richly dressed than usual, walked thence around to the front of the theater, and went in. Ascending to the dress circle, he stood for a little time gazing around upon the audience and occasionally upon the stage in his usual graceful manner. He was subsequently observed by Mr. Ford, the proprietor of the theater, to be slowly elbowing his way through the crowd that packed the rear of the dress circle toward the right side, at the extremity of which was the box where Mr. and Mrs. Lincoln and their companions were seated. Mr. Ford casually noticed this as a slightly extraordinary symptom of interest on the part of an actor so familiar with the routine of the theater and the play.

from The Life, Crime, and Capture of John Wilkes Booth by George Alfred Townsend

What does the author mean by the last two sentences?
    a. Mr. Ford was suspicious of Booth and assumed he was making his way to Mr. Lincoln's box.
    b. Mr. Ford assumed Booth's movement throughout the theater was due to being familiar with the theater.
    c. Mr. Ford thought that Booth was making his way to the theater lounge to find his companions.
    d. Mr. Ford thought that Booth was elbowing his way to the dressing room to get ready for the play.

7. When we study more carefully the effect upon the milk of the different species of bacteria found in the dairy, we find that there is a great variety of changes which they produce when they are allowed to grow in milk. The dairyman experiences many troubles with his milk. It sometimes curdles without becoming acid. Sometimes it becomes bitter, or acquires an unpleasant "tainted" taste, or, again, a "soapy" taste. Occasionally a dairyman finds his milk becoming slimy, instead of souring and curdling in the normal fashion. At such times, after a number of hours, the milk becomes so slimy that it can be drawn into long threads. Such an infection proves very troublesome, for many a time it persists in spite of all attempts made to remedy it. Again, in other cases the milk will turn blue, acquiring about the time it becomes sour a beautiful sky-blue colour. Or it may become red, or occasionally yellow. All of these troubles the dairyman owes to the presence in his milk of unusual species of bacteria which grow there abundantly.

from *The Story of Germ Life* by Herbert William Conn

What is the tone of this passage?
    a. Excitement
    b. Anger
    c. Neutral
    d. Sorrowful

8. Portland is a very beautiful city of 60,000 inhabitants, and situated on the Willamette river twelve miles from its junction with the Columbia. It is perhaps true of many of the growing cities of the West, that they do not offer the same social advantages as the older cities of the East. But this is principally the case as to what may be called boom cities, where the larger part of the population is of that floating class which follows in the line of temporary growth for the purposes of speculation, and in no sense applies to those centers of trade whose prosperity is based on the solid foundation of legitimate business. As the metropolis of a vast section of country, having broad agricultural valleys filled with improved farms, surrounded by mountains rich in mineral wealth, and boundless forests of as fine timber as the world produces, the cause of Portland's growth and prosperity is the trade which it has as the center of collection and distribution of this great wealth of natural resources, and it has attracted, not the boomer and speculator, who find their profits in the wild excitement of the boom, but the merchant, manufacturer, and investor, who seek the surer if slower channels of legitimate business and investment. These have come from the East, most of them within the last few years. They came as seeking a better and wider field to engage in the same occupations they had followed in their Eastern homes, and bringing with them all the love of polite life which they had acquired there, have established here a new society, equaling in all respects that which they left behind. Here are as fine churches, as complete a system of schools, as fine residences, as great a love of music and art, as can be found at any city of the East of equal size.

from *Oregon, Washington, and Alaska. Sights and Scenes for the Tourist*, written by E.L. Lomax in 1890

What is a characteristic of a "boom city," as indicated by the passage?
    a. A city that is built on solid business foundation of mineral wealth and farming.
    b. An area of land on the west coast that quickly becomes populated by residents from the east coast.
    c. A city that, due to the hot weather and dry climate, catches fire frequently, resulting in a devastating population drop.
    d. A city whose population is made up of people who seek quick fortunes rather than building a solid business foundation.

9. The other of the minor deities at Nemi was Virbius. Legend had it that Virbius was the young Greek hero Hippolytus, chaste and fair, who learned the art of venery from the centaur Chiron, and spent all his days in the greenwood chasing wild beasts with the virgin huntress Artemis (the Greek counterpart of Diana) for his only comrade.

from *The Golden Bough* by Sir James George Frazer

Based on a prior knowledge of literature, the reader can infer this passage is taken from which of the following?
    a. A eulogy
    b. A myth
    c. A historical document
    d. A technical document

10. When I wrote the following passages, or rather the bulk of them, I lived alone, in the woods, a mile from any neighbor, in a house which I had built myself on the shore of Walden Pond, in Concord, Massachusetts, and earned my living by the labor of my hands only. I lived there two years and two months. At present I am a sojourner in civilized life again.

from *Walden* by Henry David Thoreau

What does the word *sojourner* most likely mean at the end of the passage?
    a. Illegal alien
    b. Temporary resident
    c. Lifetime partner
    d. Farm crop

Sentence Relationships

Two underlined sentences will be given in the questions below. Then a question will be asked. Read both sentences and then choose the answer choice that best answers the question.

11. The Astros won the 2017 World Series.

The fans went wild in the streets.

What does the second sentence do?
    a. It makes an analysis of the first.
    b. It gives an example.
    c. It states an effect
    d. It provides a contrast.

12. Renewable energy means that the sources of energy used cannot be depleted.

Wind power, solar power, and biomass are types of renewable energy.

What does the second sentence do?
    a. It gives an example
    b. It expands on the first sentence.
    c. It makes a contrast.
    d. It states an effect.

13. Although the sporting goods store closed because of low traffic, their online traffic has increased over the past year.

Although their sales have increased throughout the past year, the sporting goods store closed down because they did not have high enough traffic.

How are the two sentences related?
    a. They establish a contrast.
    b. They contradict each other.
    c. They present problems and solutions.
    d. They repeat the same idea.

14. The novel *To Kill a Mockingbird* is about a trial that takes place in Maycomb, Alabama during the Great Depression.

The novel deals with issues such as rape and racial injustice.

What does the second sentence do?
    a. It reinforces the first.
    b. It states an effect.
    c. It provides a contrast.
    d. It expands on the first.

15. Recent research shows us that the biggest contributor to global warming in the past two decades is the methane gases produced from agricultural land.

We must work to reduce the biggest factor of climate change, which is carbon dioxide, by burning less fossil fuels.

How do the two sentences relate?
    a. They express roughly the same idea.
    b. They provide a cause and effect.
    c. They contradict each other.
    d. They present problems and solutions.

16. The flu virus this year is unprecedented; 20 percent of the country has fallen ill to the flu, and already 59 people have died under the age of eighteen.

This information was given to us by the CDC (Centers for Disease Control and Prevention) five days ago, although numbers might have increased since we last checked.

What does the second sentence do?
    a. It analyzes a statement made in the first.
    b. It reinforces the first.
    c. It contradicts the first.
    d. It explains what is stated in the first.

17. In response to the professor's lecture, the student added a bibliography to his essay.

Additionally, he rechecked all of his sources, making sure they were credible.

What does the second sentence do?
    a. It gives an example.
    b. It contrasts with the first.
    c. It states an effect.
    d. It expands on the first.

18. The tests show that students are less apt to learn when they have to memorize something; it shows that learning by praxis is the best way for students to retain information.

We will implement our first semester in which all subjects will be taught both in the class and outside of the class; learning by praxis will take up 30 percent of the classroom's time.

How do the two sentences relate?
    a. They provide a problem and solution.
    b. They contradict each other.
    c. They reinforce each other.
    d. They establish a contrast.

19. The Smoky Mountains have hiking and waterfalls, and they are a wonderful retreat for those who want to get away for a week or two.

My grandparents went to the Smoky Mountains last year, and they loved it; they are going back next year.

What does the second sentence do?
    a. It states an effect.
    b. It gives an example.
    c. It restates the idea found in the first.
    d. It analyzes the statement made in the first.

20. The interesting thing about painting is that one does not need the mind to enter into the process like one does in writing. With painting, it is purely creative, without the encumbrance of thought.

Painting is a very useful tool that enhances problem-solving skills and strengthens memory. One must use the mind in order to make decisions about color and texture and context along the way, so the mind is a very useful tool when it comes to painting.

What does the second sentence do?
    a. It states an effect.
    b. It proposes a solution.
    c. It makes a contrast.
    d. It expands on the first sentence.

Answer Explanations

1. A: To show the audience one of the effects of criminal rehabilitation by comparison. Choice *B* is incorrect because although it is obvious the author favors rehabilitation, the author never asks for donations from the audience. Choices *C* and *D* are also incorrect. We can infer from the passage that American prisons are probably harsher than Norway prisons. However, the best answer that captures the author's purpose is Choice *A*, because we see an effect by the author (recidivism rate of each country) comparing Norwegian and American prisons.

2. C: A sense of foreboding. The narrator, after feeling excitement for the morning, feels "that something awful was about to happen," which is considered foreboding. The narrator mentions larks and weather in the passage, but there is no proof of anger or confusion at either of them.

3. B: To convince the audience that judges holding their positions based on good behavior is a practical way to avoid corruption.

4. B: Whatever happened in his life before he had a certain internal change is irrelevant. Choices *A, C,* and *D* use some of the same language as the original passage, like "revolution," "speak," and "details," but they do not capture the meaning of the statement. The statement is saying the details of his previous life are not going to be talked about—that he had some kind of epiphany, and moving forward in his life is what the narrator cares about.

5. C: To impose a certain quality upon. The sentence states that "the impress of his dear hand [has] been stamped everywhere," regarding the quality of his tastes and creations on the house. Choice *A* is one definition of *impress*, but this definition is used more as a verb than a noun: "She impressed us as a songwriter." Choice *B* is incorrect because it is also used as a verb: "He impressed the need for something to be done." Choice *D* is incorrect because it is part of a physical act: "the businessman impressed his mark upon the envelope." The phrase in the passage is meant as figurative, since the workmen did most of the physical labor, not the Prince.

6. B: Mr. Ford assumed Booth's movement throughout the theater was due to being familiar with the theater. Choice *A* is incorrect; although Booth does eventually make his way to Lincoln's box, Mr. Ford does not make this distinction in this part of the passage. Choice *C* is incorrect; although the passage mentions "companions," it mentions Lincoln's companions rather than Booth's companions. Finally, Choice *D* is incorrect; the passage mentions "dress circle," which means the first level of the theater, but this is different from a "dressing room."

7. C: The tone of this passage is neutral since it is written in an academic/informative voice. It is important to look at the author's word choice to determine what the tone of a passage is. We have no indication that the author is excited, angry, or sorrowful at the effects of bacteria on milk, so Choices *A, B,* and *D* are incorrect.

8. D: A city whose population is made up of people who seek quick fortunes rather than building a solid business foundation. Choice *A* is a characteristic of Portland, but not that of a boom city. Choice *B* is close—a boom city is one that becomes quickly populated, but it is not necessarily always populated by residents from the east coast. Choice *C* is incorrect because a boom city is not one that catches fire frequently, but one made up of people who are looking to make quick fortunes from the resources provided on the land.

9. B: A myth. Look for the key words that give away the type of passage this is, such as "deities," "Greek hero," "centaur," and the names of demigods like Artemis. A eulogy is typically a speech given at a funeral, making Choice *A* incorrect. Choices *C* and *D* are incorrect, as "virgin huntresses" and "centaurs" are typically not found in historical or professional documents.

10. B: Temporary resident. Although we don't have much context to go off of, we know that one is probably not a "lifetime partner" or "farm crop" of civilized life. These two do not make sense, so Choices *C* and *D* are incorrect. Choice *A* is also a bit strange. To be an "illegal alien" of civilized life is not a used phrase, making Choice *A* incorrect.

11. C: The second sentence states an effect of the first sentence. The fans going wild in the streets is an effect of the Astros winning the 2017 World Series. An effect is something that is produced or something that happens because of something else that takes place.

12. A: The second sentence gives examples for the first sentence. The first sentence talks about what renewable energy is. The second sentence names the different types of renewable energy.

13. D: They repeat the same idea. Both sentences talk about the sporting goods store not having enough traffic, and that's why it closed down. Both sentences also state that the online store generated high sales throughout the past year.

14. D: The best answer is Choice *D*, that the second sentence expands on the first. We see the first sentence talk about the novel and the setting. The second sentence expands on the information of the novel by talking about what the themes are in addition to the setting.

15. C: They contradict each other. The first sentence states that it is methane gas that is the biggest contributor to climate change, while the second sentence says that carbon dioxide is the biggest factor contributing to climate change. These are contradictions.

16. B: The second sentence reinforces the first. To reinforce something means to give support. The second sentence details the evidence used to support the first sentence: facts from the CDC.

17. A: The second sentence expands on the first sentence. First, we see this expansion with the word "additionally." The sentence is expanding on what the student did in response to the professor's lecture.

18. A: The two sentences provide a problem and solution. The first sentence details the problem: students are less apt to learn when memorizing versus learning by doing. The second sentence details the solution: therefore, they are going to add more praxis into the lessons to solve this learning problem.

19. B: It gives an example. The first sentence mentions the Smoky Mountains as a vacation retreat and names some of the activities available for vacationers. The second sentence gives an example of two vacationers using the Smoky Mountains as a retreat, and how they plan to return next year.

20. C: The second sentence makes a contrast to the first. The contrast here is whether the thinking mind is important to painting. The first one says the process is "purely creative" and that the thinking mind has no place in painting; however, the second sentence tells us that problem-solving skills and memory are used in painting, and that the thinking mind is part of these behaviors.

Sentence Skills

Conventions of Standard English

Conventions of Standard English Spelling

Homophones
Homophones are words that have different meanings and spellings but sound the same. These can be confusing for English Language Learners (ELLs) and beginning students, but even native English-speaking adults can find them problematic unless informed by context. Whereas listeners must rely entirely on context to *differentiate* spoken homophone meanings, readers with good spelling knowledge have a distinct advantage since homophones are spelled differently. For instance, *their* means belonging to them; *there* indicates location; and *they're* is a contraction of *they are*; despite different meanings, they all sound the same. *Lacks* can be a plural noun or a present-tense, third-person singular verb; either way it refers to absence—*deficiencies* as a plural noun and *is deficient in* as a verb. But *lax* is an adjective that means loose, slack, relaxed, uncontrolled, or negligent. These two spellings, derivations, and meanings are completely different. With speech, listeners cannot know spelling and must use context, but with print, readers with spelling knowledge can differentiate them with or without context.

Homonyms, Homophones, and Homographs
Homophones are words that sound the same in speech but have different spellings and meanings. For example, *to, too,* and *two* all sound alike, but have three different spellings and meanings. Homophones with different spellings are also called heterographs. Homographs are words that are spelled identically but have different meanings. If they also have different pronunciations, they are heteronyms. For example, *tear* pronounced one way means a drop of liquid formed by the eye; pronounced another way, it means to rip. Homophones that are also homographs are homonyms. For example, *bark* can mean the outside of a tree or a dog's vocalization; both meanings have the same spelling. *Stalk* can mean a plant stem or to pursue and/or harass somebody; these are spelled and pronounced the same. *Rose* can mean a flower or the past tense of *rise.* Many non-linguists confuse things by using "homonym" to mean sets of words that are homophones but not homographs, and also those that are homographs but not homophones.

The word *row* can mean to use oars to propel a boat; a linear arrangement of objects or print; or an argument. It is pronounced the same with the first two meanings, but differently with the third. Because it is spelled identically regardless, all three meanings are homographs. However, the two meanings pronounced the same are homophones, whereas the one with the different pronunciation is a heteronym. By contrast, the word *read* means to peruse language, whereas the word *reed* refers to a marsh plant. Because these are pronounced the same way, they are homophones; because they are spelled differently, they are heterographs. Homonyms are both homophones and homographs—pronounced and spelled identically, but with different meanings. One distinction between homonyms is of those with separate, unrelated etymologies, called "true" homonyms, e.g. *skate* meaning a fish or *skate* meaning to glide over ice/water. Those with common origins are called polysemes or polysemous homonyms, e.g. the *mouth* of an animal/human or of a river.

Irregular Plurals
One type of irregular English plural involves words that are spelled the same whether they are singular or plural. These include *deer, fish, salmon, trout, sheep, moose, offspring, species, aircraft,* etc. The spelling rule for making these words plural is simple: they do not change. Another type of irregular English plurals does change from singular to plural form, but it does not take regular English *–s* or *–es* endings. Their

irregular plural endings are largely derived from grammatical and spelling conventions in the other languages of their origins, like Latin, German, and vowel shifts and other linguistic mutations. Some examples of these words and their irregular plurals include *child* and *children; die* and *dice; foot* and *feet; goose* and *geese; louse* and *lice; man* and *men; mouse* and *mice; ox* and *oxen; person* and *people; tooth* and *teeth;* and *woman* and *women.*

Contractions

Contractions are formed by joining two words together, omitting one or more letters from one of the component words, and replacing the omitted words with an apostrophe. An obvious yet often forgotten rule for spelling contractions is to place the apostrophe where the letters were omitted; for example, spelling errors like *did'nt* for *didn't. Didn't* is a contraction of *did not.* Therefore, the apostrophe replaces the "o" that is omitted from the "not" component. Another common error is confusing contractions with possessives because both include apostrophes, e.g. spelling the possessive *its* as "it's," which is a contraction of "it is"; spelling the possessive *their* as "they're," a contraction of "they are"; spelling the possessive *whose* as "who's," a contraction of "who is"; or spelling the possessive *your* as "you're," a contraction of "you are."

Frequently Misspelled Words

One source of spelling errors is not knowing whether to drop the final letter *e* from a word when its form is changed by adding an ending to indicate the past tense or progressive participle of a verb, converting an adjective to an adverb, a noun to an adjective, etc. Some words retain the final *e* when another syllable is added; others lose it. For example, *true* becomes *truly; argue* becomes *arguing; come* becomes *coming; write* becomes *writing;* and *judge* becomes *judging.* In these examples, the final *e* is dropped before adding the ending. But *severe* becomes *severely; complete* becomes *completely; sincere* becomes *sincerely; argue* becomes *argued;* and *care* becomes *careful.* In these examples, the final *e* is retained before adding the ending. Note that some words, like *argue* in these examples, drops the final *e* when the –*ing* ending is added to indicate the participial form; but the regular past tense ending of –*ed* makes it *argued,* in effect replacing the final *e* so that *arguing* is spelled without an *e* but *argued* is spelled with one.

Some English words contain the vowel combination of *ei,* while some contain the reverse combination of *ie.* Many people confuse these. Some examples include these:

> *ceiling, conceive, leisure, receive, weird, their, either, foreign, sovereign, neither, neighbors, seize, forfeit, counterfeit, height, weight, protein,* and *freight*

Words with *ie* include *piece, believe, chief, field, friend, grief, relief, mischief, siege, niece, priest, fierce, pierce, achieve, retrieve, hygiene, science,* and *diesel.* A rule that also functions as a mnemonic device is "I before E except after C, or when sounded like A as in 'neighbor' or 'weigh'." However, it is obvious from the list above that many exceptions exist.

Many people often misspell certain words by confusing whether they have the vowel *a, e,* or *i,* frequently in the middle syllable of three-syllable words or beginning the last syllables that sound the same in different words. For example, in the following correctly spelled words, the vowel in boldface is the one people typically get wrong by substituting one or either of the others for it:

> cem**e**tery, quant**i**ties, ben**e**fit, privil**e**ge, unpleas**a**nt, sep**a**rate, independ**e**nt, excell**e**nt, cat**e**gories, indispens**a**ble, and irrelev**a**nt

The words with final syllables that sound the same when spoken but are spelled differently include *unpleasant, independent, excellent,* and *irrelevant.* Another source of misspelling is whether or not to double consonants when adding suffixes. For example, we double the last consonant before *–ed* and *–ing* endings in *controlled, beginning, forgetting, admitted, occurred, referred,* and *hopping;* but we do not double the last consonant before the suffix in *shining, poured, sweating, loving, hating, smiling,* and *hoping.*

One way in which people misspell certain words frequently is by failing to include letters that are silent. Some letters are articulated when pronounced correctly but elided in some people's speech, which then transfers to their writing. Another source of misspelling is the converse: people add extraneous letters. For example, some people omit the silent *u* in *guarantee,* overlook the first *r* in *surprise,* leave out the *z* in *realize,* fail to double the *m* in *recommend,* leave out the middle *i* from *aspirin,* and exclude the *p* from *temperature.* The converse error, adding extra letters, is common in words like *until* by adding a second *l* at the end; or by inserting a superfluous syllabic *a* or *e* in the middle of *athletic,* reproducing a common mispronunciation.

Conventions of Standard English Punctuation

Rules of Capitalization
The first word of any document, and of each new sentence, is capitalized. Proper nouns, like names and adjectives derived from proper nouns, should also be capitalized. Here are some examples:

- Grand Canyon
- Pacific Palisades
- Golden Gate Bridge
- Freudian slip
- Shakespearian, Spenserian, or Petrarchan sonnet
- Irish song

Some exceptions are adjectives, originally derived from proper nouns, which through time and usage are no longer capitalized, like *quixotic, herculean,* or *draconian.* Capitals draw attention to specific instances of people, places, and things. Some categories that should be capitalized include the following:

- Brand names
- Companies
- Weekdays
- Months
- Governmental divisions or agencies
- Historical eras
- Major historical events
- Holidays
- Institutions
- Famous buildings
- Ships and other manmade constructions
- Natural and manmade landmarks
- Territories
- Nicknames
- Epithets
- Organizations
- Planets

- Nationalities
- Tribes
- Religions
- Names of religious deities
- Roads
- Special occasions, like the Cannes Film Festival or the Olympic Games

Exceptions

Related to American government, capitalize the noun Congress but not the related adjective congressional. Capitalize the noun U.S. Constitution, but not the related adjective constitutional. Many experts advise leaving the adjectives federal and state in lowercase, as in federal regulations or state water board, and only capitalizing these when they are parts of official titles or names, like Federal Communications Commission or State Water Resources Control Board. While the names of the other planets in the solar system are capitalized as names, Earth is more often capitalized only when being described specifically as a planet, like Earth's orbit, but lowercase otherwise since it is used not only as a proper noun but also to mean *land, ground, soil,* etc. While the name of the Bible should be capitalized, the adjective biblical should not. Regarding biblical subjects, the words heaven, hell, devil, and satanic should not be capitalized. Although race names like Caucasian, African-American, Navajo, Eskimo, East Indian, etc. are capitalized, white and black as races are not.

Names of animal species or breeds are not capitalized unless they include a proper noun. Then, only the proper noun is capitalized. Antelope, black bear, and yellow-bellied sapsucker are not capitalized. However, Bengal tiger, German shepherd, Australian shepherd, French poodle, and Russian blue cat are capitalized.

Other than planets, celestial bodies like the sun, moon, and stars are not capitalized. Medical conditions like tuberculosis or diabetes are lowercase; again, exceptions are proper nouns, like Epstein-Barr syndrome, Alzheimer's disease, and Down syndrome. Seasons and related terms like winter solstice or autumnal equinox are lowercase. Plants, including fruits and vegetables, like poinsettia, celery, or avocados, are not capitalized unless they include proper names, like Douglas fir, Jerusalem artichoke, Damson plums, or Golden Delicious apples.

Titles and Names

When official titles precede names, they should be capitalized, except when there is a comma between the title and name. But if a title follows or replaces a name, it should not be capitalized. For example, "the president" without a name is not capitalized, as in "The president addressed Congress." But with a name it is capitalized, like "President Obama addressed Congress." Or, "Chair of the Board Janet Yellen was appointed by President Obama." One exception is that some publishers and writers nevertheless capitalize President, Queen, Pope, etc., when these are not accompanied by names to show respect for these high offices. However, many writers in America object to this practice for violating democratic principles of equality. Occupations before full names are not capitalized, like owner Mark Cuban, director Martin Scorsese, or coach Roger McDowell.

Some universal rules for capitalization in composition titles include capitalizing the following:

- The first and last words of the title
- Forms of the verb *to be* and all other verbs
- Pronouns
- The word *not*

Universal rules for NOT capitalizing in titles include the articles *the, a,* or *an;* the conjunctions *and, or,* or *nor,* and the preposition *to,* or *to* as part of the infinitive form of a verb. The exception to all of these is UNLESS any of them is the first or last word in the title, in which case they are capitalized. Other words are subject to differences of opinion and differences among various stylebooks or methods. These include *as, but, if,* and *or,* which some capitalize and others do not. Some authorities say no preposition should ever be capitalized; some say prepositions five or more letters long should be capitalized. The *Associated Press Stylebook* advises capitalizing prepositions longer than three letters (like *about, across,* or *with*).

Ellipses

Ellipses (. . .) signal omitted text when quoting. Some writers also use them to show a thought trailing off, but this should not be overused outside of dialogue. An example of an ellipses would be if someone is quoting a phrase out of a professional source but wants to omit part of the phrase that isn't needed: "Dr. Skim's analysis of pollen inside the body is clearly a myth . . . that speaks to the environmental guilt of our society."

Commas

Commas separate words or phrases in a series of three or more. The Oxford comma is the last comma in a series. Many people omit this last comma, but many times it causes confusion. Here is an example:

I love my sisters, the Queen of England and Madonna.

This example without the comma implies that the "Queen of England and Madonna" are the speaker's sisters. However, if the speaker was trying to say that they love their sisters, the Queen of England, as well as Madonna, there should be a comma after "Queen of England" to signify this.

Commas also separate two coordinate adjectives ("big, heavy dog") but not cumulative ones, which should be arranged in a particular order for them to make sense ("beautiful ancient ruins").

A comma ends the first of two independent clauses connected by conjunctions. Here is an example:

I ate a bowl of tomato soup, and I was hungry very shortly after.

Here are some brief rules for commas:

- Commas follow introductory words like *however, furthermore, well, why,* and *actually,* among others.
- Commas go between city and state: Houston, Texas.
- If using a comma between a surname and Jr. or Sr. or a degree like M.D., also follow the whole name with a comma: "Martin Luther King, Jr., wrote that."
- A comma follows a dependent clause beginning a sentence: "Although she was very small, . . ."
- Nonessential modifying words/phrases/clauses are enclosed by commas: "Wendy, who is Peter's sister, closed the window."
- Commas introduce or interrupt direct quotations: "She said, 'I hate him.' 'Why,' I asked, 'do you hate him?'"

Semicolons

Semicolons are used to connect two independent clauses but should never be used in the place of a comma. They can replace periods between two closely connected sentences: "Call back tomorrow; it can wait until then." When writing items in a series and one or more of them contains internal commas, separate them with semicolons, like the following:

People came from Springfield, Illinois; Alamo, Tennessee; Moscow, Idaho; and other locations.

Hyphens

Here are some rules concerning hyphens:

- Compound adjectives like state-of-the-art or off-campus are hyphenated.
- Original compound verbs and nouns are often hyphenated, like "throne-sat," "video-gamed," "no-meater."
- Adjectives ending in *–ly* are often hyphenated, like "family-owned" or "friendly-looking."
- "Five years old" is not hyphenated, but singular ages like "five-year-old" are.
- Hyphens can clarify. For example, in "stolen vehicle report," "stolen-vehicle report" clarifies that "stolen" modifies "vehicle," not "report."
- Compound numbers twenty-one through ninety-nine are spelled with hyphens.
- Prefixes before proper nouns/adjectives are hyphenated, like "mid-September" and "trans-Pacific."

Parentheses

Parentheses enclose information such as an aside or more clarifying information: "She ultimately replied (after deliberating for an hour) that she was undecided." They are also used to insert short, in-text definitions or acronyms: "His FBS (fasting blood sugar) was higher than normal." When parenthetical information ends the sentence, the period follows the parentheses: "We received new funds ($25,000)." Only put periods within parentheses if the whole sentence is inside them: "Look at this. (You'll be astonished.)" However, this can also be acceptable as a clause: "Look at this (you'll be astonished)." Although parentheses appear to be part of the sentence subject, they are not, and do not change subject-verb agreement: "Will (and his dog) was there."

Quotation Marks

Quotation marks are typically used when someone is quoting a direct word or phrase someone else writes or says. Additionally, quotation marks should be used for the titles of poems, short stories, songs, articles, chapters, and other shorter works. When quotations include punctuation, periods and commas should *always* be placed inside of the quotation marks.

When a quotation contains another quotation inside of it, the outer quotation should be enclosed in double quotation marks and the inner quotation should be enclosed in single quotation marks. For example: "Timmy was begging, 'Don't go! Don't leave!'" When using both double and single quotation marks, writers will find that many word-processing programs may automatically insert enough space between the single and double quotation marks to be visible for clearer reading. But if this is not the case, the writer should write/type them with enough space between to keep them from looking like three single quotation marks. Additionally, non-standard usages, terms used in an unusual fashion, and technical terms are often clarified by quotation marks. Here are some examples:

My "friend," Dr. Sims, has been micromanaging me again.

This way of extracting oil has been dubbed "fracking."

Apostrophes

One use of the apostrophe is followed by an *s* to indicate possession, like *Mrs. White's home* or *our neighbor's dog*. When using the *'s* after names or nouns that also end in the letter *s,* no single rule applies: some experts advise adding both the apostrophe and the *s*, like "the Jones's house," while others prefer using only the apostrophe and omitting the additional *s*, like "the Jones' house." The wisest expert advice is to pick one formula or the other and then apply it consistently. Newspapers and magazines often use *'s* after common nouns ending with *s*, but add only the apostrophe after proper nouns or names ending with *s*. One common error is to place the apostrophe before a name's final *s* instead of after it: "Ms. Hasting's book" is incorrect if the name is Ms. Hastings.

Plural nouns should not include apostrophes (e.g. "apostrophe's"). Exceptions are to clarify atypical plurals, like verbs used as nouns: "These are the do's and don'ts." Irregular plurals that do not end in *s* always take apostrophe-*s*, not *s*-apostrophe—a common error, as in "childrens' toys," which should be "children's toys." Compound nouns like mother-in-law, when they are singular and possessive, are followed by apostrophe-*s*, like "your mother-in-law's coat." When a compound noun is plural and possessive, the plural is formed before the apostrophe-*s*, like "your sisters-in-laws' coats." When two people named possess the same thing, use apostrophe-*s* after the second name only, like "Dennis and Pam's house."

Sentence Structures

Incomplete Sentences
Four types of incomplete sentences are sentence fragments, run-on sentences, subject-verb and/or pronoun-antecedent disagreement, and non-parallel structure.

Sentence fragments are caused by absent subjects, absent verbs, or dangling/uncompleted dependent clauses. Every sentence must have a subject and a verb to be complete. An example of a fragment is "Raining all night long," because there is no subject present. "It was raining all night long" is one correction. Another example of a sentence fragment is the second part in "Many scientists think in unusual ways. Einstein, for instance." The second phrase is a fragment because it has no verb. One correction is "Many scientists, like Einstein, think in unusual ways." Finally, look for "cliffhanger" words like *if, when, because,* or *although* that introduce dependent clauses, which cannot stand alone without an independent clause. For example, to correct the sentence fragment "If you get home early," add an independent clause: "If you get home early, we can go dancing."

Run-On Sentences
A run-on sentence combines two or more complete sentences without punctuating them correctly or separating them. For example, a run-on sentence caused by a lack of punctuation is the following:

> There is a malfunction in the computer system however there is nobody available right now who knows how to troubleshoot it.

One correction is, "There is a malfunction in the computer system; however, there is nobody available right now who knows how to troubleshoot it." Another is, "There is a malfunction in the computer system. However, there is nobody available right now who knows how to troubleshoot it."

An example of a comma splice of two sentences is the following:

> Jim decided not to take the bus, he walked home.

Replacing the comma with a period or a semicolon corrects this. Commas that try and separate two independent clauses without a contraction are considered comma splices.

Parallel Sentence Structures

Parallel structure in a sentence matches the forms of sentence components. Any sentence containing more than one description or phrase should keep them consistent in wording and form. Readers can easily follow writers' ideas when they are written in parallel structure, making it an important element of correct sentence construction. For example, this sentence lacks parallelism: "Our coach is a skilled manager, a clever strategist, and works hard." The first two phrases are parallel, but the third is not. Correction: "Our coach is a skilled manager, a clever strategist, and a hard worker." Now all three phrases match in form. Here is another example:

Fred intercepted the ball, escaped tacklers, and a touchdown was scored.

This is also non-parallel. Here is the sentence corrected:

Fred intercepted the ball, escaped tacklers, and scored a touchdown.

Sentence Fluency

For fluent composition, writers must use a variety of sentence types and structures, and also ensure that they smoothly flow together when they are read. To accomplish this, they must first be able to identify fluent writing when they read it. This includes being able to distinguish among simple, compound, complex, and compound-complex sentences in text; to observe variations among sentence types, lengths, and beginnings; and to notice figurative language and understand how it augments sentence length and imparts musicality. Once students/writers recognize superior fluency, they should revise their own writing to be more readable and fluent. They must be able to apply acquired skills to revisions before being able to apply them to new drafts.

One strategy for revising writing to increase its sentence fluency is flipping sentences. This involves rearranging the word order in a sentence without deleting, changing, or adding any words. For example, the student or other writer who has written the sentence, "We went bicycling on Saturday" can revise it to, "On Saturday, we went bicycling." Another technique is using appositives. An appositive is a phrase or word that renames or identifies another adjacent word or phrase. Writers can revise for sentence fluency by inserting main phrases/words from one shorter sentence into another shorter sentence, combining them into one longer sentence, e.g. from "My cat Peanut is a gray and brown tabby. He loves hunting rats." to "My cat Peanut, a gray and brown tabby, loves hunting rats." Revisions can also connect shorter sentences by using conjunctions and commas and removing repeated words: "Scott likes eggs. Scott is allergic to eggs" becomes "Scott likes eggs, but he is allergic to them."

One technique for revising writing to increase sentence fluency is "padding" short, simple sentences by adding phrases that provide more details specifying why, how, when, and/or where something took place. For example, a writer might have these two simple sentences: "I went to the market. I purchased a cake." To revise these, the writer can add the following informative dependent and independent clauses and prepositional phrases, respectively: "Before my mother woke up, I sneaked out of the house and went to the supermarket. As a birthday surprise, I purchased a cake for her." When revising sentences to make them longer, writers must also punctuate them correctly to change them from simple sentences to compound, complex, or compound-complex sentences.

Skills Writers Can Employ to Increase Fluency

One way writers can increase fluency is by varying the beginnings of sentences. Writers do this by starting most of their sentences with different words and phrases rather than monotonously repeating the same ones across multiple sentences. Another way writers can increase fluency is by varying the lengths of sentences. Since run-on sentences are incorrect, writers make sentences longer by also converting them from simple to compound, complex, and compound-complex sentences. The coordination and subordination involved in these also give the text more variation and interest, hence more fluency. Here are a few more ways writers can increase fluency:

- Varying the transitional language and conjunctions used makes sentences more fluent.
- Writing sentences with a variety of rhythms by using prepositional phrases.
- Varying sentence structure adds fluency.

Knowledge of Language

Use Grammar to Enhance Clarity in Writing

Possessives

Possessive forms indicate possession, i.e. that something belongs to or is owned by someone or something. As such, the most common parts of speech to be used in possessive form are adjectives, nouns, and pronouns. The rule for correctly spelling/punctuating possessive nouns and proper nouns is with -'s, like "the woman's briefcase" or "Frank's hat." With possessive adjectives, however, apostrophes are not used: these include *my, your, his, her, its, our,* and *their,* like "my book," "your friend," "his car," "her house," "its contents," "our family," or "their property." Possessive pronouns include *mine, yours, his, hers, its, ours,* and *theirs.* These also have no apostrophes. The difference is that possessive adjectives take direct objects, whereas possessive pronouns replace them. For example, instead of using two possessive adjectives in a row, as in "I forgot my book, so Blanca let me use her book," which reads monotonously, replacing the second one with a possessive pronoun reads better: "I forgot my book, so Blanca let me use hers."

Pronouns

There are three pronoun cases: subjective case, objective case, and possessive case. Pronouns as subjects are pronouns that replace the subject of the sentence, such as *I, you, he, she, it, we, they* and *who.* Pronouns as objects replace the object of the sentence, such as *me, you, him, her, it, us, them,* and *whom.* Pronouns that show possession are *mine, yours, hers, its, ours, theirs,* and *whose.* The following are examples of different pronoun cases:

- Subject pronoun: *She* ate the cake for her birthday. *I* saw the movie.
- Object pronoun: You gave *me* the card last weekend. She gave the picture to *him.*
- Possessive pronoun: That bracelet you found yesterday is *mine. His* name was Casey.

Adjectives

Adjectives are descriptive words that modify nouns or pronouns. They may occur before or after the nouns or pronouns they modify in sentences. For example, in "This is a big house," *big* is an adjective modifying or describing the noun *house.* In "This house is big," the adjective is at the end of the sentence rather than preceding the noun it modifies.

A rule of punctuation that applies to adjectives is to separate a series of adjectives with commas. For example, "Their home was a large, rambling, old, white, two-story house." A comma should never separate the last adjective from the noun, though.

Adverbs

Whereas adjectives modify and describe nouns or pronouns, adverbs modify and describe adjectives, verbs, or other adverbs. Adverbs can be thought of as answers to questions in that they describe when, where, how, how often, how much, or to what extent.

Many (but not all) adjectives can be converted to adverbs by adding –*ly*. For example, in "She is a quick learner," *quick* is an adjective modifying *learner*. In "She learns quickly," *quickly* is an adverb modifying *learns*. One exception is *fast*. *Fast* is an adjective in "She is a fast learner." However, –*ly* is never added to the word *fast*; it retains the same form as an adverb in "She learns fast."

Verbs

A verb is a word or phrase that expresses action, feeling, or state of being. Verbs explain what their subject is *doing*. Three different types of verbs used in a sentence are action verbs, linking verbs, and helping verbs.

Action verbs show a physical or mental action. Some examples of action verbs are *play, type, jump, write, examine, study, invent, develop,* and *taste*. The following example uses an action verb:

Kat *imagines* that she is a mermaid in the ocean.

The verb *imagines* explains what Kat is doing: she is imagining being a mermaid.

Linking verbs connect the subject to the predicate without expressing an action. The following sentence shows an example of a linking verb:

The mango *tastes* sweet.

The verb *tastes* is a linking verb. The mango doesn't *do* the tasting, but the word *taste* links the mango to its predicate, sweet. Most linking verbs can also be used as action verbs, such as *smell, taste, look, seem, grow,* and *sound*. Saying something *is* something else is also an example of a linking verb. For example, if we were to say, "Peaches is a dog," the verb *is* would be a linking verb in this sentence, since it links the subject to its predicate.

Helping verbs are verbs that help the main verb in a sentence. Examples of helping verbs are *be, am, is, was, have, has, do, did, can, could, may, might, should,* and *must*, among others. The following are examples of helping verbs:

Jessica *is* planning a trip to Hawaii.

Brenda *does* not like camping.

Xavier *should* go to the dance tonight.

Notice that after each of these helping verbs is the main verb of the sentence: *planning, like,* and *go.* Helping verbs usually show an aspect of time.

Transitional Words and Phrases

In connected writing, some sentences naturally lead to others, whereas in other cases, a new sentence expresses a new idea. We use transitional phrases to connect sentences and the ideas they convey. This makes the writing coherent. Transitional language also guides the reader from one thought to the next. For example, when pointing out an objection to the previous idea, starting a sentence with "However," "But," or "On the other hand" is transitional. When adding another idea or detail, writers use "Also," "In addition," "Furthermore," "Further," "Moreover," "Not only," etc. Readers have difficulty perceiving connections between ideas without such transitional wording.

Subject-Verb Agreement

Lack of subject-verb agreement is a very common grammatical error. One of the most common instances is when people use a series of nouns as a compound subject with a singular instead of a plural verb. Here is an example:

> Identifying the best books, locating the sellers with the lowest prices, and paying for them *is* difficult

instead of saying "*are* difficult." Additionally, when a sentence subject is compound, the verb is plural:

> He and his cousins *were* at the reunion.

However, if the conjunction connecting two or more singular nouns or pronouns is "or" or "nor," the verb must be singular to agree:

> That pen or another one like it is in the desk drawer.

If a compound subject includes both a singular noun and a plural one, and they are connected by "or" or "nor," the verb must agree with the subject closest to the verb: "Sally or her sisters go jogging daily"; but "Her sisters or Sally goes jogging daily."

Simply put, singular subjects require singular verbs and plural subjects require plural verbs. A common source of agreement errors is not identifying the sentence subject correctly. For example, people often write sentences incorrectly like, "The group of students *were* complaining about the test." The subject is not the plural "students" but the singular "group." Therefore, the correct sentence should read, "The group of students *was* complaining about the test." The converse also applies, for example, in this incorrect sentence: "The facts in that complicated court case *is* open to question." The subject of the sentence is not the singular "case" but the plural "facts." Hence the sentence would correctly be written: "The facts in that complicated court case *are* open to question." New writers should not be misled by the distance between the subject and verb, especially when another noun with a different number intervenes as in these examples. The verb must agree with the subject, not the noun closest to it.

Pronoun-Antecedent Agreement

Pronouns within a sentence must refer specifically to one noun, known as the *antecedent*. Sometimes, if there are multiple nouns within a sentence, it may be difficult to ascertain which noun belongs to the pronoun. It's important that the pronouns always clearly reference the nouns in the sentence so as not to confuse the reader. Here's an example of an unclear pronoun reference:

> After Catherine cut Libby's hair, David bought her some lunch.

The pronoun in the examples above is *her*. The pronoun could either be referring to *Catherine* or *Libby*. Here are some ways to write the above sentence with a clear pronoun reference:

> After Catherine cut Libby's hair, David bought Libby some lunch.

> David bought Libby some lunch after Catherine cut Libby's hair.

But many times the pronoun will clearly refer to its antecedent, like the following:

> After David cut Catherine's hair, he bought her some lunch.

Vocabulary Acquisition

Context Clues

Readers can often figure out what unfamiliar words mean without interrupting their reading to look them up in dictionaries by examining context. Context includes the other words or sentences in a passage. One common context clue is the root word and any affixes (prefixes/suffixes). Another common context clue is a synonym or definition included in the sentence. Sometimes both exist in the same sentence. Here's an example:

> Scientists who study birds are *ornithologists*.

Many readers may not know the word *ornithologist*. However, the example contains a definition (scientists who study birds). The reader may also have the ability to analyze the suffix (*-logy*, meaning the study of) and root (*ornitho-*, meaning bird).

Another common context clue is a sentence that shows differences. Here's an example:

> Birds *incubate* their eggs outside of their bodies, unlike mammals.

Some readers may be unfamiliar with the word *incubate*. However, since we know that "unlike mammals," birds incubate their eggs outside of their bodies, we can infer that *incubate* has something to do with keeping eggs warm outside the body until they are hatched.

In addition to analyzing the etymology of a word's root and affixes and extrapolating word meaning from sentences that contrast an unknown word with an antonym, readers can also determine word meanings from sentence context clues based on logic. Here's an example:

> Birds are always looking out for predators that could attack their young.

The reader who is unfamiliar with the word *predator* could determine from the context of the sentence that predators usually prey upon baby birds and possibly other young animals. Readers might also use the context clue of etymology here, as *predator* and *prey* have the same root.

Analyzing Word Parts

By learning some of the etymologies of words and their parts, readers can break new words down into components and analyze their combined meanings. For example, the root word *soph* is Greek for wise or knowledge. Knowing this informs the meanings of English words including *sophomore, sophisticated,* and *philosophy.* Those who also know that *phil* is Greek for love will realize that *philosophy* means the love of knowledge. They can then extend this knowledge of *phil* to understand *philanthropist* (one who loves people), *bibliophile* (book lover), *philharmonic* (loving harmony), *hydrophilic* (water-loving), and so on. In addition, *phob-* derives from the Greek *phobos,* meaning fear. This informs all words ending with it as meaning fear of various things: *acrophobia* (fear of heights), *arachnophobia* (fear of spiders), *claustrophobia* (fear of enclosed spaces), *ergophobia* (fear of work), *homophobia* (fear of homosexuality), and *hydrophobia* (fear of water), among others.

Some English word origins from other languages, like ancient Greek, are found in large numbers and varieties of English words. An advantage of the shared ancestry of these words is that once readers recognize the meanings of some Greek words or word roots, they can determine or at least get an idea of what many different English words mean. As an example, the Greek word *métron* means to measure, a measure, or something used to measure; the English word meter derives from it. Knowing this informs many other English words, including *altimeter, barometer, diameter, hexameter, isometric,* and *metric.* While readers must know the meanings of the other parts of these words to decipher their meaning fully, they already have an idea that they are all related in some way to measures or measuring.

While all English words ultimately derive from a proto-language known as Indo-European, many of them historically came into the developing English vocabulary later, from sources like the ancient Greeks' language, the Latin used throughout Europe and much of the Middle East during the reign of the Roman Empire, and the Anglo-Saxon languages used by England's early tribes. In addition to classic revivals and native foundations, by the Renaissance era other influences included French, German, Italian, and Spanish. Today we can often discern English word meanings by knowing common roots and affixes, particularly from Greek and Latin.

The following is a list of common prefixes and their meanings:

Prefix	Definition	Examples
a-	without	atheist, agnostic
ad-	to, toward	advance
ante-	before	antecedent, antedate
anti-	opposing	antipathy, antidote
auto-	self	autonomy, autobiography
bene-	well, good	benefit, benefactor
bi-	two	bisect, biennial
bio-	life	biology, biosphere
chron-	time	chronometer, synchronize
circum-	around	circumspect, circumference
com-	with, together	commotion, complicate
contra-	against, opposing	contradict, contravene
cred-	belief, trust	credible, credit
de-	from	depart
dem-	people	demographics, democracy
dis-	away, off, down, not	dissent, disappear
equi-	equal, equally	equivalent
ex-	former, out of	extract
for-	away, off, from	forget, forswear
fore-	before, previous	foretell, forefathers
homo-	same, equal	homogenized
hyper-	excessive, over	hypercritical, hypertension
in-	in, into	intrude, invade
inter-	among, between	intercede, interrupt
mal-	bad, poorly, not	malfunction
micr-	small	microbe, microscope
mis-	bad, poorly, not	misspell, misfire
mono-	one, single	monogamy, monologue
mor-	die, death	mortality, mortuary
neo-	new	neolithic, neoconservative

non-	not	nonentity, nonsense
omni-	all, everywhere	omniscient
over-	above	overbearing
pan-	all, entire	panorama, pandemonium
para-	beside, beyond	parallel, paradox
phil-	love, affection	philosophy, philanthropic
poly-	many	polymorphous, polygamous
pre-	before, previous	prevent, preclude
prim-	first, early	primitive, primary
pro-	forward, in place of	propel, pronoun
re-	back, backward, again	revoke, recur
sub-	under, beneath	subjugate, substitute
super-	above, extra	supersede, supernumerary
trans-	across, beyond, over	transact, transport
ultra-	beyond, excessively	ultramodern, ultrasonic, ultraviolet
un-	not, reverse of	unhappy, unlock
vis-	to see	visage, visible

The following is a list of common suffixes and their meanings:

Suffix	Definition	Examples
-able	likely, able to	capable, tolerable
-ance	act, condition	acceptance, vigilance
-ard	one that does excessively	drunkard, wizard
-ation	action, state	occupation, starvation
-cy	state, condition	accuracy, captaincy
-er	one who does	teacher
-esce	become, grow, continue	convalesce, acquiesce
-esque	in the style of, like	picturesque, grotesque
-ess	feminine	waitress, lioness
-ful	full of, marked by	thankful, zestful
-ible	able, fit	edible, possible, divisible
-ion	action, result, state	union, fusion
-ish	suggesting, like	churlish, childish
-ism	act, manner, doctrine	barbarism, socialism
-ist	doer, believer	monopolist, socialist
-ition	action, result, state,	sedition, expedition
-ity	quality, condition	acidity, civility
-ize	cause to be, treat with	sterilize, mechanize, criticize
-less	lacking, without	hopeless, countless
-like	like, similar	childlike, dreamlike
-ly	like, of the nature of	friendly, positively
-ment	means, result, action	refreshment, disappointment
-ness	quality, state	greatness, tallness
-or	doer, office, action	juror, elevator, honor
-ous	marked by, given to	religious, riotous

-some	apt to, showing	tiresome, lonesome
-th	act, state, quality	warmth, width
-ty	quality, state	enmity, activity

Practice Questions

Sentence Correction

Select the choice you think best fits the underlined part of the sentence. If the original is the best answer choice, then choose Choice A.

1. After getting a cat, Billy <u>learned the meaning of</u> take care of something other than himself.
    a. learned the meaning of
    b. learned what it meant to
    c. meant to learning the
    d. made to learn of the

2. A toothache does not always denote tooth decay or a cavity; sometimes <u>it was the direct</u> result of having a sinus infection.
    a. it was the direct
    b. it be the direct
    c. it directly was
    d. it is the direct

3. <u>Play baseball, swimming, and dancing</u> are three of Hannah's favorite ways to be active.
    a. Play baseball, swimming, and dancing
    b. Playing baseball; swimming; dancing;
    c. Playing baseball, to swim and to dance,
    d. Playing baseball, swimming, and dancing

4. <u>I was shocked by the sound of the blast muting</u> the television and went outside to see what happened.
    a. I was shocked by the sound of the blast muting
    b. I was shocked by the sound of the blast, muted
    c. Shocked at the sound of the blast, I muted
    d. The sound of the blast shocked me, muting

5. <u>The dog turned in a circle five times before its tail</u> went between its legs and it went to sleep.
    a. The dog turned in a circle five times before its tail
    b. For the dog, it turned around five times before its tail
    c. A dog's turning in a circle five times before its tail
    d. The dog turned in a circle five times before their tail

6. <u>The food at the fashion show being the best part</u>, which was shipped in from twenty different countries and prepared by world-renowned chefs.
    a. The food at the fashion show being the best part
    b. The best part about being at the fashion show was the food
    c. At the fashion show the food was the best part of the party,
    d. The best part of the fashion show been the food,

7. Every time the mosquito truck came driving down the road with the poison, <u>the kids riding their bikes behind it</u>.
  a. the kids riding their bikes behind it.
  b. the kids' rode their bikes' behind it.
  c. the kids would ride their bikes behind it.
  d. the kids rides their bikes behind it.

8. <u>Gertrude is fearful and worried about her sister coming into</u> town because she knows there will be a lot of work to do.
  a. Gertrude is fearful and worried about her sister coming into
  b. Gertrude is worried about and fearful her sister coming into
  c. Gertrude is fearful, worried about her sister coming into
  d. Gertrude is fearful of and worried about her sister coming into

9. <u>Before they decided on Costa Rica for their honeymoon</u>, the couple researched at least eight other vacation spots in different countries.
  a. Before they decided on Costa Rica for their honeymoon
  b. They decided on Costa Rica for their honeymoon
  c. Before their honeymoon, deciding on Costa Rica,
  d. Costa Rica as their honeymoon,

10. On the first day of school, <u>Kayla, late to three of her classes,</u> and never found the fourth!
  a. Kayla, late to three of her classes,
  b. Kayla being late to three of her classes
  c. Kayla to three of her classes late
  d. Kayla was late to three of her classes

Construction Shift

In the following questions, rewrite the sentence following the directions. The new sentence should retain the meaning of the original sentence, and it should also be clear and straightforward.

11. We cancelled our vacation to California due to the destruction of the wildfires.

Rewrite, beginning with:

<u>Due to the destruction of the wildfires,</u>

The next words will be
  a. our vacation to California was cancelled.
  b. the vacation to California being cancelled.
  c. cancelling of the vacation in California.
  d. the California vacation is cancelling.

12. The sun came out, and everyone went outside to sunbathe.

Rewrite, beginning with:

Everyone went outside to sunbathe

The next words will be
    a. and the sun came out.
    b. despite the sun.
    c. started to get sunny.
    d. when the sun came out.

13. Although it was dark outside, Marie went swimming.

Rewrite, beginning with:

Marie went swimming

The next words will be
    a. because it was dark outside.
    b. if it was dark outside.
    c. even though it was dark outside.
    d. and it was dark outside.

14. We went to the store, and then we went bowling.

Rewrite, beginning with:

We went bowling

The next words will be
    a. although we went to the store.
    b. before we went to the store.
    c. after we went to the store.
    d. because we went to the store.

15. It was surprising to find Cameron at the dog park, since he did not own a dog.

Rewrite, beginning with:

Cameron did not own a dog,

The next words will be
    a. but it was surprising
    b. so it was surprising
    c. though it was surprising
    d. yet it was surprising

16. If she knew what she was getting into, Karen would not have joined the debate club.

Rewrite, beginning with:

<u>Karen joined the debate club</u>

The next words will be
     a. without knowledge of
     b. with knowledge of
     c. having the knowledge of
     d. getting into the knowledge of

17. The freezing weather made them doubt whether they wanted to go hiking next week.

Rewrite, beginning with:

<u>They did not want to go hiking next week</u>

The next words will be
     a. later the freezing weather
     b. despite the freezing whether
     c. due to the freezing weather
     d. therefore the freezing whether

18. Cats come alive when it gets dark outside.

Rewrite, beginning with:

<u>It gets dark outside,</u>

The next words will be
     a. and then cats
     b. when cats
     c. since cats
     d. but then cats

19. If I knew I was going to receive such a warm welcome, I wouldn't have been so nervous!

Rewrite, beginning with:

<u>Being nervous was pointless,</u>

The next words will be
     a. not knowing I received
     b. a warm welcome received
     c. I was going to receive
     d. knowing that I received

20. Though this was not the case one year ago, this year has been a happy one!

Rewrite, beginning with:

<u>This has been a happy year,</u>

The next words will be
    a. unless last year
    b. although last year
    c. because of last year
    d. unlike last year

Answer Explanations

1. B: The correct answer is Choice *B*: "Billy learned what it meant to take care of something other than himself." Choice *A* is awkwardly worded and doesn't flow with the rest of the sentence. Choice *C*, "meant to learning" is also incorrect because it is missing a "to" after the phrase, and the word "learning" is also in the wrong verb form. Choice *D* is also worded awkwardly and thus the latter part of the sentence is unclear with this phrase.

2. D: The sentence should read: "sometimes it is the direct result of having a sinus infection." Choice *A* is incorrect because "was" is in past tense, and the rest of the sentence is in present tense. Choice *B* is incorrect because "it be" is not proper subject/verb agreement. "Be" should be conjugated to "is" as a be-verb. Finally, Choice *C* is incorrect; we have a past tense "was" which is incorrect, we are missing the article "the," and it is poorly worded.

3. D: Choice *D* is the best answer choice because the gerunds are all in parallel structure: "Playing baseball, swimming, and dancing." Choice *A* is incorrect because "Play baseball" does not match the parallel structure of the other two gerunds. Choice *B* is incorrect because the answer uses semicolons instead of commas, which is incorrect. Semicolons are used to separate independent clauses. Choice *C* is incorrect because "to swim" and "to dance" eschew parallel structure.

4. C: The correct answer is Choice *C*: "Shocked at the sound of the blast, I muted the television and went outside to see what happened." Choice *A* is incorrect because we're not sure if it is the "I" that's doing the muting or the blast. Choice *B* has incorrect sentence structure. We have "I was shocked" and that carries over to "I was muted," which is incorrect. We need someone doing the muting without the helping verb. Choice *D* is incorrect; we don't have a proper subject to go with the verb "muting." "Me muting" is not correct. Right now, it's the "sound" that's doing the muting, and this is incorrect.

5. A: Choice *A* is the best answer because it is the most straightforward. Choice *B* adds "For the dog, it turned around," which makes the sentence more confusing than the simple, "The dog turned in a circle." Choice *C* is incorrect because "A dog turned" is clearer subject/verb agreement than "A dog's turning," which does not match the other verb tense. Choice *D* is incorrect pronoun agreement; "their" should be "its" because there is only one dog.

6. B: Choice *B* is the correct answer choice. Choice *A* is incorrect because the verb "being" is incorrect usage; it should say "the food was the best part," not "the food being the best part." Choice *C* is incorrect because the way the sentence is worded, it seems as if the "party" was shipped from twenty different countries, not the "food"; it has a misplaced modifier. Choice *D* is incorrect; it is missing the helping verb "has."

7. C: Choice *C* is the best answer choice because we have an independent clause with correct subject/verb agreement. Choice *A* does not have an independent clause, due to the verb form "riding," which should be "would ride." Choice *B* is incorrect; "kids" and "bikes" are plural and show no possession of anything, so there should be no apostrophes behind those words. Choice *D* is incorrect; "kids rides" is incorrect subject/verb agreement. The correct phrase should be "kids ride."

8. D: Choice *D* is the best answer choice because it uses parallelism in its prepositions: "fearful of" and "worried about." Choice *A* is incorrect because one wouldn't be "fearful about" something, but "fearful of" something. Choice *B* is incorrect; the preposition after fearful is missing altogether. Choice *C* is incorrect because a comma doesn't belong in between "fearful" and "worried." This does not correct the problem of still needing a preposition after "fearful."

9. A: The answer choice is correct as-is because it is a dependent clause connected to an independent clause and contains the correct subject-verb agreement and clarity. Choice *B* is incorrect because if we were to place this sentence before the last sentence, we would have two independent clauses separated by a comma, and this would create a comma splice. Choice *C* is incorrect; this is not the best answer because it isn't the clearest, since the subject "they" or "the couple" comes later in the sentence. Choice *D* is incorrect because the phrasing is awkward and not as clear as Choice *A*.

10. D: Choice *D* is the best answer because it has the proper subject/verb agreement: "Kayla was late." Choice *A* is incorrect because there is no helping verb before "late," and the comma separates the next phrase which should be the verbal phrase. Choice *B* is incorrect because the verb is not the right form; it should be "was late" not "being late." Choice *C* is incorrect because the word order is inverted.

11. A: Due to the destruction of the wildfires, our vacation to California was cancelled. Choice *B* is incorrect because the verb "being" should be "was." Choice *C* is incorrect because there is no subject to go with the verb "cancelling"; the noun "vacation" is in a prepositional phrase, which does not count as a subject. Choice *D* is incorrect because "is cancelling" denotes a continuous action, and we know that it just got cancelled once.

12. D: Choice *D* is the best answer: "Everyone went outside to sunbathe when the sun came out" is the closest in meaning to the original. Choice *A* is incorrect because the order is switched around. The original sentence implies that the sun came out *first*, and we don't see that in Choice *A*. Choice *B* is incorrect because it changes the meaning; people went out *because of* the sun, not *despite* it. Choice *C* is correct because it does not form a dependent clause or a complex sentence; "started to get sunny" is not a proper phrase to tack onto an independent clause.

13. C: The original sentence tells us that even though it was dark outside, Marie went swimming, so the correct answer is Choice *C*. Choice *A* is incorrect because it changes the meaning; Marie went swimming *although* it was dark outside, not *because*. Choice *B* is also incorrect; we are not told Marie goes swimming "if it is dark outside." Choice *D* is incorrect; this may be true, but it's not *as close* to the original meaning as Choice *C* is.

14. C: Choice *C* is the best answer choice because it is consistent with the chronological order depicted in the original sentence. Choice *A* is incorrect because this changes the meaning; there is no contrast in the original sentence like the word "although" in Choice *A*. Choice *B* is incorrect because this changes the order of the original sentence. Choice *D* is incorrect; this changes the meaning of the original sentence.

15. B: The correct answer is: "Cameron did not own a dog, so it was surprising to find him at the dog park." Choices *A* and *D* mean essentially the same thing. There is no "but" or "yet" contrast indicated in the original sentence. Choice *C* is incorrect, because "though" means "although" or "even though," and this is also not indicated in the original sentence.

16. A: The best answer choice is the following: "Karen joined the debate club without knowledge of what she was getting into." Choices *B* and *C* are incorrect because we know from the original sentence that Karen had *no knowledge* of what she was getting into. Choice *D* is incorrect; this does not fit with the sentence structure.

17. C: The best answer choice is *C*: "They did not want to go hiking next week due to the freezing weather." We know that it's the freezing weather that made them doubt their initial plans to go hiking. Choice *A* is incorrect; the word "later" isn't a proper transition word. Choice *B* is incorrect; they didn't want to go hiking *because of* the freezing weather, not *despite* it. Choice *D* is incorrect; the word "therefore" doesn't make sense in this context.

18. A: The best answer is Choice *A*: "It gets dark outside, and then cats come alive." Choice *B* is incorrect because it insinuates that it gets dark outside *after* cats come alive, and this is not the case. Choice *C* is also incorrect, because it doesn't get dark outside *since cats* come alive. Choice *D* is also incorrect; adding "but" implies a contrast, and there is no contrast here.

19. D: Choice *D* is the best answer choice: "Being nervous was pointless, knowing that I received such a warm welcome." Choice *A* is the opposite of the correct answer; being nervous was pointless because they *knew* they were going to receive a warm welcome. Choice *B* is incorrect; let's look at it in the sentence: "Being nervous was pointless, a warm welcome received . . . " This is not as clear as Choice *D*. Choice *C* would create two independent clauses with a comma splice, so this is also incorrect.

20. D: The best answer is Choice *D*. "This has been a happy year, unlike last year," effectively sums up the meaning of the original sentence. Choice *A* is incorrect; "unless last year" does not reflect the meaning of the original sentence. Choice *B* is incorrect; "although last year" does not reflect the original meaning either. Choice *C* is incorrect; "because of last year" contradicts the original meaning.

WritePlacer

Argument Structure and Organization

When authors write text for the purpose of persuading others to agree with them, they assume a position with the subject matter about which they are writing. Rather than presenting information objectively, the author treats the subject matter subjectively so that the information presented supports his or her position. In their argumentation, the author presents information that refutes or weakens opposing positions. Another technique authors use in persuasive writing is to anticipate arguments against the position. When students learn to read subjectively, they gain experience with the concept of persuasion in writing and learn to identify positions taken by authors. This enhances their reading comprehension and develops their skills for identifying pro and con arguments and biases.

There are five main parts of the classical argument that writers employ in a well-designed stance:

- Introduction: In the introduction to a classical argument, the author establishes goodwill and rapport with the reading audience, warms up the readers, and states the thesis or general theme of the argument.

- Narration: In the narration portion, the author gives a summary of pertinent background information, informs the readers of anything they need to know regarding the circumstances and environment surrounding and/or stimulating the argument, and establishes what is at risk or the stakes in the issue or topic. Literature reviews are common examples of narrations in academic writing.

- Confirmation: The confirmation states all claims supporting the thesis and furnishes evidence for each claim, arranging this material in logical order—e.g. from most obvious to most subtle or strongest to weakest.

- Refutation and Concession: The refutation and concession discuss opposing views and anticipate reader objections without weakening the thesis, yet permitting as many oppositions as possible.

- Summation: The summation strengthens the argument while summarizing it, supplying a strong conclusion and showing readers the superiority of the author's solution.

Introduction

A classical argument's introduction must pique reader interest, get readers to perceive the author as a writer, and establish the author's position. Shocking statistics, new ways of restating issues, or quotations or anecdotes focusing the text can pique reader interest. Personal statements, parallel instances, or analogies can also begin introductions—so can bold thesis statements if the author believes readers will agree. Word choice is also important for establishing author image with readers. For example, readers will respond differentially whether a writer discussing abortion uses terms like "pro-family supporters" or "people opposed to abortion" or terms like "pro-lifers." The introduction should typically narrow down to a clear, sound thesis statement. If readers cannot locate one sentence in the introduction explicitly stating the writer's position or the point they support, the writer probably has not refined the introduction sufficiently.

Narration and Confirmation

The narration part of a classical argument should create a context for the argument by explaining the issue to which the argument is responding, and by supplying any background information that influences the issue. Readers should understand the issues, alternatives, and stakes in the argument by the end of the narration to enable them to evaluate the author's claims equitably. The confirmation part of the classical argument enables the author to explain why they believe in the argument's thesis. The author builds a chain of reasoning by developing several individual supporting claims and explaining why that evidence supports each claim and also supports the overall thesis of the argument.

Refutation and Concession and Summation

The classical argument is the model for argumentative/persuasive writing, so authors often use it to establish, promote, and defend their positions. In the refutation aspect of the refutation and concession part of the argument, authors disarm reader opposition by anticipating and answering their possible objections, persuading them to accept the author's viewpoint. In the concession aspect, authors can concede those opposing viewpoints with which they agree. This can avoid weakening the author's thesis while establishing reader respect and goodwill for the author: all refutation and no concession can antagonize readers who disagree with the author's position. In the conclusion part of the classical argument, a less skilled writer might simply summarize or restate the thesis and related claims; however, this does not provide the argument with either momentum or closure. More skilled authors revisit the issues and the narration part of the argument, reminding readers of what is at stake.

Formal and Informal Language

Formal language is less personal than informal language. It is more "buttoned-up" and business-like, adhering to proper grammatical rules. It is used in professional or academic contexts, to convey respect or authority. For example, one would use formal language to write an informative or argumentative essay for school or to address a superior. Formal language avoids contractions, slang, colloquialisms, and first-person pronouns. Formal language uses sentences that are usually more complex and often in passive voice. Punctuation can differ as well. For example, *exclamation points (!)* are used to show strong emotion or can be used as an *interjection* but should be used sparingly in formal writing situations.

Informal language is often used when communicating with family members, friends, peers, and those known more personally. It is more casual, spontaneous, and forgiving in its conformity to grammatical rules and conventions. Informal language is used for personal emails and correspondence between coworkers or other familial relationships. The tone is more relaxed. In informal writing, slang, contractions, clichés, and the first- and second-person are often used.

Elements of the Writing Process

Skilled writers undergo a series of steps that comprise the writing process. The purpose of adhering to a structured approach to writing is to develop clear, meaningful, coherent work.

The stages are pre-writing or planning, organizing, drafting/writing, revising, and editing. Not every writer will necessarily follow all five stages for every project but will judiciously employ the crucial components of the stages for most formal or important work. For example, a brief informal response to a short reading passage may not necessitate the need for significant organization after idea generation, but larger assignments and essays will likely mandate use of the full process.

Pre-Writing/Planning

Brainstorming

One of the most important steps in writing is pre-writing. Before drafting an essay or other assignment, it's helpful to think about the topic for a moment or two, in order to gain a more solid understanding of what the task is. Then, spend about five minutes jotting down the immediate ideas that could work for the essay. Brainstorming is a way to get some words on the page and offer a reference for ideas when drafting. Scratch paper is provided for writers to use any pre-writing techniques such as webbing, freewriting, or listing. Some writers prefer using graphic organizers during this phase. The goal is to get ideas out of the mind and onto the page.

Freewriting

Like brainstorming, freewriting is another prewriting activity to help the writer generate ideas. This method involves setting a timer for two or three minutes and writing down all ideas that come to mind about the topic using complete sentences. Once time is up, writers should review the sentences to see what observations have been made and how these ideas might translate into a more unified direction for the topic. Even if sentences lack sense as a whole, freewriting is an excellent way to get ideas onto the page in the very beginning stages of writing. Using complete sentences can make this a bit more challenging than brainstorming, but overall it is a worthwhile exercise, as it may force the writer to come up with more complete thoughts about the topic.

Once the ideas are on the page, it's time for the writer to turn them into a solid plan for the essay. The best ideas from the brainstorming results can then be developed into a more formal outline.

Organizing

Although sometimes it is difficult to get going on the brainstorming or prewriting phase, once ideas start flowing, writers often find that they have amassed too many thoughts that will not make for a cohesive and unified essay. During the organization stage, writers should examine the generated ideas, hone in on the important ones central to their main idea, and arrange the points in a logical and effective manner. Writers may also determine that some of the ideas generated in the planning process need further elaboration, potentially necessitating the need for research to gather infortmation to fill the gaps.

Once a writer has chosen his or her thesis and main argument, selected the most applicable details and evidence, and eliminated the "clutter," it is time to strategically organize the ideas. This is often accomplished with an outline.

Outlining

An *outline* is a system used to organize writing. When composing essays, outlining is important because it helps writers organize important information in a logical pattern using Roman numerals. Usually, outlines start out with the main ideas and then branch out into subgroups or subsidiary thoughts or subjects. Not only do outlines provide a visual tool for writers to reflect on how events, ideas, evidence, or other key parts of the argument relate to one another, but they can also lead writers to a stronger conclusion.

The sample below demonstrates what a general outline looks like:

- I. Introduction
  - 1. Background
  - 2. Thesis statement
- II. Body
  - 1. Point A
    - a. Supporting evidence
    - b. Supporting evidence
  - 2. Point B
    - a. Supporting evidence
    - b. Supporting evidence
  - 3. Point C
    - a. Supporting evidence
    - b. Supporting evidence
- III. Conclusion
  - 1. Restate main points of the paper.
  - 2. End with something memorable.

Drafting/Writing

Now it comes time to actually write the essay. In this stage, writers should follow the outline they developed in the brainstorming process and try to incorporate the useful sentences penned in the freewriting exercise. The main goal of this phase is to put all the thoughts together in cohesive sentences and paragraphs.

It is helpful for writers to remember that their work here does not have to be perfect. This process is often referred to as *drafting* because writers are just creating a rough draft of their work. Because of this, writers should avoid getting bogged down on the small details.

Referencing Sources

Anytime a writer quotes or paraphrases another text, they will need to include a citation. A citation is a short description of the work that a quote or information came from. The style manual your teacher wants you to follow will dictate exactly how to format that citation. For example, this is how one would cite a book according to the APA manual of style:

- *Format:* Last name, First initial, Middle initial. (Year Published) *Book Title.* City, State: Publisher.
- *Example:* Sampson, M. R. (1989). *Diaries from an alien invasion.* Springfield, IL: Campbell Press.

Revising

Revising offers an opportunity for writers to polish things up. Putting one's self in the reader's shoes and focusing on what the essay actually says helps writers identify problems—it's a movement from the mindset of writer to the mindset of editor. The goal is to have a clean, clear copy of the essay.

The main goal of the revision phase is to improve the essay's flow, cohesiveness, readability, and focus. For example, an essay will make a less persuasive argument if the various pieces of evidence are scattered and presented illogically or clouded with unnecessary thought. Therefore, writers should consider their essay's structure and organization, ensuring that there are smooth transitions between sentences and paragraphs. There should be a discernable introduction and conclusion as well, as these crucial components of an essay provide readers with a blueprint to follow.

Additionally, if the writer includes copious details that do little to enhance the argument, they may actually distract readers from focusing on the main ideas and detract from the strength of their work. The ultimate goal is to retain the purpose or focus of the essay and provide a reader-friendly experience. Because of this, writers often need to delete parts of their essay to improve its flow and focus. Removing sentences, entire paragraphs, or large chunks of writing can be one of the toughest parts of the writing process because it is difficult to part with work one has done. However, ultimately, these types of cuts can significantly improve one's essay.

Lastly, writers should consider their voice and word choice. The voice should be consistent throughout and maintain a balance between an authoritative and warm style, to both inform and engage readers. One way to alter voice is through word choice. Writers should consider changing weak verbs to stronger ones and selecting more precise language in areas where wording is vague. In some cases, it is useful to modify sentence beginnings or to combine or split up sentences to provide a more varied sentence structure.

Editing

Rather than focusing on content (as is the aim in the revising stage), the editing phase is all about the mechanics of the essay: the syntax, word choice, and grammar. This can be considered the proofreading stage. Successful editing is what sets apart a messy essay from a polished document.

The following areas should be considered when proofreading:

- Sentence fragments
- Awkward sentence structure
- Run-on sentences
- Incorrect word choice
- Grammatical agreement errors
- Spelling errors
- Punctuation errors
- Capitalization errors

One of the most effective ways of identifying grammatical errors, awkward phrases, or unclear sentences is to read the essay out loud. Listening to one's own work can help move the writer from simply the author to the reader.

During the editing phase, it's also important to ensure the essay follows the correct formatting and citation rules as dictated by the assignment.

Recursive Writing Process

While the writing process may have specific steps, the good news is that the process is recursive, meaning the steps need not be completed in a particular order. Many writers find that they complete steps at the same time such as drafting and revising, where the writing and rearranging of ideas occur simultaneously or in very close order. Similarly, a writer may find that a particular section of a draft needs more development and will go back to the prewriting stage to generate new ideas. The steps can be repeated at any time, and the more these steps of the recursive writing process are employed, the better the final product will be.

Practice Makes Prepared Writers

Like any other useful skill, writing only improves with practice. While writing may come more easily to some than others, it is still a skill to be honed and improved. Regardless of a person's natural abilities, there is always room for growth in writing. Practicing the basic skills of writing can aid in preparations for the exam.

One way to build vocabulary and enhance exposure to the written word is through reading. This can be through reading books, but reading of any materials such as newspapers, magazines, and even social media count towards practice with the written word. This also helps to enhance critical reading and thinking skills, through analysis of the ideas and concepts read. Think of each new reading experience as a chance to sharpen these skills.

Developing a Well-Organized Paragraph

A paragraph is a series of connected and related sentences addressing one topic. Writing good paragraphs benefits writers by helping them to stay on target while drafting and revising their work. It benefits readers by helping them to follow the writing more easily. Regardless of how brilliant their ideas may be, writers who do not present them in organized ways will fail to engage readers—and fail to accomplish their writing goals. A fundamental rule for paragraphing is to confine each paragraph to a single idea. When writers find themselves transitioning to a new idea, they should start a new paragraph. However, a paragraph can include several pieces of evidence supporting its single idea; and it can include several points if they are all related to the overall paragraph topic. When writers find each point becoming lengthy, they may choose instead to devote a separate paragraph to every point and elaborate upon each more fully.

An effective paragraph should have these elements:

- Unity: One major discussion point or focus should occupy the whole paragraph from beginning to end.

- Coherence: For readers to understand a paragraph, it must be coherent. Two components of coherence are logical and verbal bridges. In logical bridges, the writer may write consecutive sentences with parallel structure or carry an idea over across sentences. In verbal bridges, writers may repeat key words across sentences.

- A topic sentence: The paragraph should have a sentence that generally identifies the paragraph's thesis or main idea.

- Sufficient development: To develop a paragraph, writers can use the following techniques after stating their topic sentence:

    o Define terms
    o Cite data
    o Use illustrations, anecdotes, and examples
    o Evaluate causes and effects
    o Analyze the topic
    o Explain the topic using chronological order

A topic sentence identifies the main idea of the paragraph. Some are explicit, some implicit. The topic sentence can appear anywhere in the paragraph. However, many experts advise beginning writers to place each paragraph topic sentence at or near the beginning of its paragraph to ensure that their readers understand what the topic of each paragraph is. Even without having written an explicit topic sentence, the writer should still be able to summarize readily what subject matter each paragraph addresses. The writer must then fully develop the topic that is introduced or identified in the topic sentence. Depending on what the writer's purpose is, they may use different methods for developing each paragraph.

Two main steps in the process of organizing paragraphs and essays should both be completed after determining the writing's main point, while the writer is planning or outlining the work. The initial step is to give an order to the topics addressed in each paragraph. Writers must have logical reasons for putting one paragraph first, another second, etc. The second step is to sequence the sentences in each paragraph. As with the first step, writers must have logical reasons for the order of sentences. Sometimes the work's main point obviously indicates a specific order.

Topic Sentences

To be effective, a topic sentence should be concise so that readers get its point without losing the meaning among too many words. As an example, in *Only Yesterday: An Informal History of the 1920s* (1931), author Frederick Lewis Allen's topic sentence introduces his paragraph describing the 1929 stock market crash: "The Bull Market was dead." This example illustrates the criteria of conciseness and brevity. It is also a strong sentence, expressed clearly and unambiguously. The topic sentence also introduces the paragraph, alerting the reader's attention to the main idea of the paragraph and the subject matter that follows the topic sentence.

Experts often recommend opening a paragraph with the topic sentences to enable the reader to realize the main point of the paragraph immediately. Application letters for jobs and university admissions also benefit from opening with topic sentences. However, positioning the topic sentence at the end of a paragraph is more logical when the paragraph identifies a number of specific details that accumulate evidence and then culminates with a generalization. While paragraphs with extremely obvious main ideas need no topic sentences, more often—and particularly for students learning to write—the topic sentence is the most important sentence in the paragraph. It not only communicates the main idea quickly to readers; it also helps writers produce and control information.

Writing Prompt

In response to the following prompt, write a 300- to 600-word essay.

Substance abuse recovery centers in Florida have doubled in the past two years. Additionally, the centers that already existed are filled to the maximum occupancy. In order to accommodate the patients, some recovery centers are expanding their residencies and adding more staff. The reason for this rise in recovery centers speaks to the state of our nation with the abuse of drugs and alcohol. The substance abuse problem is worse than ever before and will only continue to grow if we allow the trafficking and consumption of drugs to go unpunished.

Write a response in which you identify your stance on the argument above. Once you've identified your stance, use concrete evidence to support your argument.

Greetings!

First, we would like to give a huge "thank you" for choosing us and this study guide for your ACCUPLACER exam. We hope that it will lead you to success on this exam and for your years to come.

Our team has tried to make your preparations as thorough as possible by covering all of the topics you should be expected to know. In addition, our writers attempted to create practice questions identical to what you will see on the day of your actual test. We have also included many test-taking strategies to help you learn the material, maintain the knowledge, and take the test with confidence.

We strive for excellence in our products, and if you have any comments or concerns over the quality of something in this study guide, please send us an email so that we may improve.

As you continue forward in life, we would like to remain alongside you with other books and study guides in our library. We are continually producing and updating study guides in several different subjects. If you are looking for something in particular, all of our products are available on Amazon. You may also send us an email!

Sincerely,
APEX Test Prep
info@apexprep.com

FREE

Free Study Tips DVD

In addition to the tips and content in this guide, we have created a FREE DVD with helpful study tips to further assist your exam preparation. **This FREE Study Tips DVD provides you with top-notch tips to conquer your exam and reach your goals.**

Our simple request in exchange for the strategy-packed DVD is that you email us your feedback about our study guide. We would love to hear what you thought about the guide, and we welcome any and all feedback—positive, negative, or neutral. It is our #1 goal to provide you with top quality products and customer service.

To receive your **FREE Study Tips DVD**, email freedvd@apexprep.com. Please put "FREE DVD" in the subject line and put the following in the email:

    a. The name of the study guide you purchased.

    b. Your rating of the study guide on a scale of 1-5, with 5 being the highest score.

    c. Any thoughts or feedback about your study guide.

    d. Your first and last name and your mailing address, so we know where to send your free DVD!

Thank you!

Made in the USA
Middletown, DE
24 July 2019